THE LAW OF PREMISES LIABILITY

by
Margaret C. Jasper

Oceana's Legal Almanac Series
Law for the Layperson

2000
Oceana Publications, Inc.
Dobbs Ferry, New York

Information contained in this work has been obtained by Oceana Publications from sources believed to be reliable. However, neither the Publisher nor its authors guarantee the accuracy or completeness of any information published herein, and neither Oceana nor its authors shall be responsible for any errors, omissions or damages arising from the use of this information. This work is published with the understanding that Oceana and its authors are supplying information, but are not attempting to render legal or other professional services. If such services are required, the assistance of an appropriate professional should be sought.

Library of Congress Control Number: 00-134128

ISBN 0-379-11347-3

Oceana's Legal Almanac Series: Law for the Layperson
ISSN 1075-7376

©2000 by Oceana Publications, Inc.

Manufactured in the United States of America on acid-free paper.

To My Husband Chris

Your love and support
are my motivation and inspiration

-and-

In memory of my son, Jimmy

Table of Contents

CHAPTER 3:
PREMISES LIABILITY LITIGATION

CHAPTER 4:
SPECIAL CONSIDERATIONS

CHAPTER 5:
THE PREMISES SECURITY CLAIM

CHAPTER 6:
GOVERNMENTAL IMMUNITY

APPENDICES

ABOUT THE AUTHOR

MARGARET C. JASPER is an attorney engaged in the general practice of law in South Salem, New York, concentrating in the areas of personal injury and entertainment law. Ms. Jasper holds a Juris Doctor degree from Pace University School of Law, White Plains, New York, is a member of the New York and Connecticut bars, and is certified to practice before the United States District Courts for the Southern and Eastern Districts of New York, and the United States Supreme Court.

Ms. Jasper has been appointed to the panel of arbitrators of the American Arbitration Association and the law guardian panel for the Family Court of the State of New York, is a member of the Association of Trial Lawyers of America, and is a New York State licensed real estate broker and member of the Westchester County Board of Realtors, operating as Jasper Real Estate, in South Salem, New York.

Ms. Jasper is the author and general editor of the following legal almanacs: Juvenile Justice and Children's Law; Marriage and Divorce; Estate Planning; The Law of Contracts; The Law of Dispute Resolution; Law for the Small Business Owner; The Law of Personal Injury; Real Estate Law for the Homeowner and Broker; Everyday Legal Forms; Dictionary of Selected Legal Terms; The Law of Medical Malpractice; The Law of Product Liability; The Law of No-Fault Insurance; The Law of Immigration; The Law of Libel and Slander; The Law of Buying and Selling; Elder Law; The Right to Die; AIDS Law; The Law of Obscenity and Pornography; The Law of Child Custody; The Law of Debt Collection; Consumer Rights Law; Bankruptcy Law for the Individual Debtor; Victim's Rights Law; Animal Rights Law; Workers' Compensation Law; Employee Rights in the Workplace; Probate Law; Environmental Law; Labor Law; The Americans with Disabilities Act; The Law of Capital Punishment; Education Law; The Law of Violence Against Women; Landlord-Tenant Law; Insurance Law; Religion and the Law; Commercial Law; Motor Vehicle Law; Social Security Law; The Law of Drunk Driving; The Law of Speech and the First Amendment;

Employment Discrimination Under Title VII; Hospital Liability Law; Home Mortgage Law Primer; Copyright Law; Patent Law; Trademark Law; Special Education Law; Premises Liability Law; and The Law of Attachment and Garnishment.

INTRODUCTION

This legal almanac explores the area of law known generally as "premises liability." If an individual has an accident or sustains injuries on "premises" which are owned or maintained by someone else, liability may attach if those injuries are the result of a dangerous condition existing on the property.

Property owners and business establishments have a duty to provide a safe environment for individuals on their premises. If an individual is injured because a property owner or a business establishment failed to provide a safe environment, the injured person has a right to bring a claim for their pain and suffering, medical expenses and lost wages.

For example, a common premises liability case involves a "slip and fall" in a supermarket. If the fall is the result of the supermarket's negligence—e.g. in failing to keep the floor clean of debris—the injured person has a right to recover their medical expenses, and damages for their pain and suffering, and other related costs. One's spouse may also be able to recover money damages for loss of the injured spouse's services.

This almanac presents an overview of premises liability law, and the various types of premises liability claims, including premises security claims, the elements necessary to prove the case, the defenses, insurance issues, governmental immunity, and damages.

The Appendix provides sample documents, applicable statutes, and other pertinent information and data. The Glossary contains definitions of many of the terms used throughout the almanac.

CHAPTER 1:
OVERVIEW

IN GENERAL

Premises liability is an area of personal injury law that is concerned with injuries sustained on premises which are owned or maintained by another as a result of a dangerous or unsafe condition located on that property. A premises liability claim may arise at a place of business, or in the home or on the property of another. For example, an individual may "slip and fall" on a slippery floor in the supermarket, or twist their ankle in a pothole. Liability may also attach if an individual is harmed by a third person due to a lack of security on the premises.

As further discussed in this almanac, in order to prevail in a premises liability lawsuit, the owner of the property must have been negligent in some way which caused an unsafe condition on the property, and the injuries must have been "caused" by this unsafe or dangerous condition. For example, if the owner can prove that you were at fault for your fall, depending upon the jurisdiction, this evidence may reduce or even eliminate your ability to recover for your injuries.

In addition, the extent of the injuries must also be evaluated to decide whether they are reasonably compensable. If one falls and scrapes his or her knee as a result of debris negligently left in the aisle of a department store, although the store may be liable, the injuries are not serious enough to warrant initiating a lawsuit because the damages are negligible.

TRENDS IN UNINTENTIONAL INJURIES IN THE UNITED STATES

The National Center for Injury Prevention and Control (NCIPC), through its Division of Unintentional Injury Prevention, monitors trends in unintentional injuries in the United States, conducts research to better understand risk factors, and evaluates interventions to prevent these injuries.

According to the NCIPC, unintentional injuries are the leading cause of death in the United States for people aged 1-34. Each year, more than 90,000 people die in the U.S. as a result of unintentional injuries and unintentional injuries account for nearly 31 million emergency room visits.

According to the National Safety Council (NSC), a fatal injury occurs every 6 minutes and a disabling injury occurs every 2 seconds in the United States. In 1998, there were 92,200 deaths caused by unintentional injuries. This was a 5% decrease from 1988, when the death total reached 97,100.

Wage losses, medical expenses, property damages, employer costs, fire losses and other expenses related to unintentional injuries and fatalities cost Americans an estimated $480.5 billion in 1998.

Causes

The leading causes of fatal unintentional injuries in 1998 were the same top five since 1970 and they account for 80% of all deaths—i.e., 74,000 of the 92,200. The majority of unintentional injury deaths were caused by motor vehicle accidents, which totalled 41,200 in 1998. The second highest cause of unintentional injury deaths were falls, which totalled 16,600. Poisoning deaths totalled 8,400. Drowning deaths totalled 4,100 and deaths due to fires and burns totalled 3,700.

Injuries in the Home

According to the NSC, there were 28,200 fatalities and 6,800,000 disabling injuries in 1998 which occurred in the home—a fatal injury every 19 minutes and a disabling injury every 5 seconds—which were unintentional. The four leading fatal events were falls, solid and liquid poisonings, fires and burns, and suffocation by an ingested object. The leading cause of death in the home was due to falls, which took the lives of 10,700 people in 1998—a 9 percent increase over 1996, when there occurred 9,800 fatal falls in the home.

NSC recommendations for reducing deaths and injuries in the home include safety precautions to reduce the risk of falls in the home, especially if elderly people live or visit the home, paying particular attention to the staircases, which account for the majority of fall injuries in the home. In addition, a fire escape plan should be developed in case of fire or other emergency. Smoke detectors and fire extinguishers should be installed in case of fire, and the smoke detector batteries should be checked regularly.

Injuries in the Community

According to the NSC, there were 20,000 fatalities in 1998 due to unintentional injuries, including deaths which occurred in public places. This total did not include motor vehicle or work-related accidents. The number of public unintentional injury deaths increased by 500, or 3%, between 1997 and 1998—one death occurring every 26 minutes. Disabling injuries occur one every 5 seconds. The five leading causes of fatal public injuries are falls, drowning, water, air and railroad transportation.

NSC recommendations for reducing deaths and injuries in the community include making communities walkable by providing residents access to safe walking areas. In particular, children should have safe walking routes to school. Initiatives to address recreational safety should also be increased. Finally, the NSC recommends that all adults learn CPR and first aid techniques to give assistance if an injury does occur.

Workplace Injuries

According to the NSC, there were 5,100 workplace fatalities in 1998 due to unintentional injuries—one every 103 minutes. In addition, 3.8 million American workers suffered from disabling injuries on the job—one every 8 seconds. The four leading fatal events and exposures are highway traffic incidents, homicide, falls to a lower level, and being struck by an object. The agricultural industry accounted for 780 deaths and 140,000 disabling injuries in 1998. Agricultural workers had the second highest death rate among the major industry divisions.

Work injuries cost Americans $125.1 billion in 1998—equivalent to nearly triple the combined profits reported by the top 5 Fortune 500 companies in 1998.

To address this problem, Congress has made a number of recommendations to increase safety in the workplace, and has advocated that employers should operate with a comprehensive safety and health plan and address security issues that can prevent workplace violence.

Worker's Compensation Insurance

An employer who maintains workers' compensation insurance coverage for his or her employees is generally immune from employee lawsuits for work-related injuries. Thus, if you are injured at work, your injuries will most likely be handled through your state worker's compensation program. In that case, you would be precluded from taking any action against your employer for money damages above what you would receive under the worker's compensation insurance program.

The workers' compensation system was established so that disabled employees would not risk financial ruin and the uncertainty of a lawsuit. Employers benefit by avoiding the time and expense of litigation by making sure their workers receive benefits for work-related disabilities.

Because workers' compensation is designed to cover a disabled worker's economic losses, most state workers' compensation programs provide the following benefits: (i) wage loss compensation; (ii) medical benefits; and (iii) rehabilitation benefits.

Third Party Claims

Although the employer is generally immune from liability under workers' compensation law, the employee maintains his or her right to sue any negligent third parties who may have caused or contributed to their injury. For example, if an independently contracted construction company working at the employer's place of business negligently left a hole in the floor uncovered, and an employee stepped in the hole and broke his ankle, the employee may be able to sue the construction company even though the accident occurred at the workplace.

For a more detailed discussion of the worker's compensation system, the reader is advised to consult this author's legal almanac entitled Worker's Compensation Law, also published by Oceana Publishing Company.

Dog Attacks

Every year, 4.7 million people are bitten by dogs and 800,000 of those bitten require medical attention. According to the NCIPC, someone seeks medical care because of a dog bite every 40 seconds. Thus, each year 1.8% of the U.S. population is bitten by a dog, and 0.3% of the U.S. population seeks medical care for a bite. In 1986, dog bites were the 12th leading cause of non-fatal injuries for all age groups in the United States. Studies show that biting dogs were more likely to be male, unneutered, and chained.

If an individual is injured by a dog on your premises, you may be liable to the injured person. Generally, the court will only apply strict liability upon the owner where a dog has previously bitten another person without provocation. In such a case, the rules of negligence would not apply because the owner would have been on notice that the dog was dangerous and needed to be confined.

Otherwise, in order to prevail, the plaintiff must generally demonstrate that the dog had vicious propensities and that the owner knew or should have known of those propensities. The owner's "knowledge" of the animal's vicious propensity may be inferred from the circumstances surrounding the incident. For example, if the owner trained the dog as a guard dog, it could be inferred that the owner was aware that the dog was likely to attack a stranger on the property. In addition, certain breeds of dogs have been deemed vicious by nature. Owners of those breeds of dogs—e.g., the pit bull—are deemed to have constructive notice of the animal's vicious propensities.

The owner of the dog may be able to assert a contributory or comparative negligence defense if the injured person was somehow responsible for the attack—e.g., where the individual was teasing or otherwise provoking the dog into action. In that case, the injured party's damages may be reduced or eliminated, depending on the comparative negligence rules of the jurisdiction.

These are general principles. Insofar as case law is inconsistent in this area, and statutes may vary among the jurisdictions, the reader is advised to check the law of his or her own jurisdiction concerning specific animal liability issues.

Staircase Injuries

In premises liability cases, stairs are a known and common cause of an individual's fall and subsequent injuries. Lighting and corrective measures to the actual stairs are two of the aspects of safety design that are most likely to reduce accidents and, thus, liability.

Obvious defects in stairs include torn or loose carpets, or a broken step or rail, and liability is easy to prove. However, there are some stair defects that are not so obvious. Thus, in bringing a lawsuit based on a staircase injury, one may have to carefully examine the staircase to determine how the injury occurred and how the stairs could have been constructed and/or maintained in a safer condition in order to hold another responsible for the accident.

Some of the less obvious conditions contributing to falls include a worn area on the section of the stair that most often connects with the foot, which would make it more slippery than the rest of the stair. In addition, a buildup of snow or ice on an outdoor staircase can be very dangerous. Outdoor stairs must be built and maintained so that there is no unnecessary buildup which poses a danger—e.g., an anti-slip surface.

Most building codes require stairways to have one or more handrails on stairs of a certain width or a certain height because reaching for a handrail which is at the wrong height can actually cause a person to fall. Building codes also set forth the maximum and minimum riser height for each step, and the maximum and minimum depth of the run, as well as the maximum variance from one step to another. Oftentimes, an accident is caused because the stair has not met these requirements, thus making the staircase defective.

If a staircase fails to comply with a building code requirement, this would constitute a statutory violation, and the owner may be deemed "negligent per se," in which case the plaintiff need only prove that the owner violated the building code, thus creating a rebuttable presumption that the owner was negligent.

Statutory violations are discussed further in Chapter 3 of this almanac.

Environmental Hazards

Premises liability may also stem from environmental hazards existing on the premises for which the owner may be liable. For example, landlords may be liable for tenant health problems caused by exposure to environmental hazards, such as asbestos. The Occupational Safety and Health Administration (OSHA) has issued strict standards for the testing, maintenance and disclosure of asbestos in buildings constructed before 1981. For further information, OSHA may be reached by telephone at: (202) 219-8148 or at their internet website: http://www.osha.gov.

In addition, as further discussed in Chapter 4, federal legislation has been enacted to address the problem of lead poisoning in children caused by lead-based paint.

CHAPTER 2:
THE PREMISES LIABILITY CLAIM

IN GENERAL

If you are on someone else's property and injure yourself as a result of a dangerous condition on the property, the owner or possessor of the property may be liable for your injuries. On the other hand, if you are a property owner and someone injures himself on your land, you may find yourself legally responsible for his or her injuries.

SEEK MEDICAL TREATMENT

If you are the injured party, you should immediately seek medical treatment. Even if you do not believe you have been seriously harmed, oftentimes an injury is not immediately discernable, such as a back injury. If you fall and believe you require medical attention, call an ambulance. Do not try to be a martyr and make it to the hospital on your own or with the help of friends or relatives. This could be dangerous, particularly if you sustain a head, neck or back injury.

In addition, the ambulance attendants are obligated to create a medical record which will help support your claim as to the time, date and occurrence of your injury. It is important to medically document your injury as close to the time it occurred as possible. A long lapse between the occurrence and medical treatment always raises questions as to whether there was any intervening injury that caused the medical condition.

DOCUMENT THE INCIDENT

As soon as practicable following the accident, you should document the facts and gather evidence in case you decide in the future that you are entitled to pursue a premises liability claim against the party responsible for your injuries.

You should put the owner or possessor of the property on notice. For example, if the accident occurred in a store, file a written report with the manager on duty. Make sure the facts are accurate and request a copy of the incident report at the time it is made.

Obtain the names, addresses and telephone numbers of any witnesses to the accident, as well as any individuals who saw you immediately after the accident occurred. Even though they did not see you actually fall, they could still testify to your physical condition following the fall and the circumstances surrounding the accident, e.g. lighting, condition of floor, etc.

If there is any physical evidence that contributed to your accident, or which demonstrates your injuries—e.g., blood-soaked clothing—you should try to preserve that evidence. If the evidence is not within your control, you should take photographs, e.g., a broken step. Make sure that you clearly label the photographs with the date and time they were taken. The developer can imprint the date on the back of the prints as proof of the date the film was developed.

In addition, you should write down all of the circumstances surrounding the accident while the facts are still fresh in your mind, including the manner in which you were injured. Small but important facts can fade in your memory over time, such as comments made by a witness or the responsible party. Keep a journal of the progression of your pain, your symptoms and injuries. It is also important to keep track of how much time you lost at work or school, and any other physical limitations caused by the accident, e.g., the amount of time spent in the hospital, and confined to your home and/or bed.

RETAIN AN ATTORNEY

When a claim is relatively simple and straightforward, there may be no need to retain a lawyer. However, if your injuries are serious and/or have caused you any significant damages, including lost wages, medical expenses, etc., you should contact an attorney who will investigate the facts surrounding the incident, and will evaluate whether you have a viable premises liability claim. You may also need to retain an attorney in cases where the insurance carrier is simply acting in bad faith and won't deal fairly with you.

At your first meeting with your prospective attorney, take with you the documentation and evidence you previously gathered. This will assist the attorney in investigating your case, and make it more likely that the attorney will take the case and be able to obtain a favorable settlement or verdict on your behalf.

Prior to taking any action on a case, an attorney will typically require the client to sign a retainer agreement. A retainer agreement is a contract between the lawyer and the client, which sets forth their understanding. It details the responsibilities the lawyer is agreeing to undertake and the compensation the lawyer expects to receive if there is a recovery, by verdict or settlement.

Most personal injury retainer agreements are contingency fee agreements. This means that the client does not have to pay any money towards legal fees up front to the lawyer in order for the lawyer to take on the case. In return, the lawyer receives a percentage—typically one-third—of the recovery, if there is one. If there is no recovery, the lawyer basically forgoes the legal fee. A personal injury lawyer may also advance some or all of the costs of the case, which are then deducted from the verdict or settlement amount.

A sample retainer agreement in a premises liability case is set forth at Appendix 1.

Your attorney will contact the appropriate insurance carrier for the responsible party, and place them on notice that your claim exists. The date, place and manner in which the claim arose will be provided to the insurance carrier, as well as a copy of any police, ambulance, hospital, and/or medical reports, to the extent available at that time.

A claims representative from the owner's insurance company may call to take a statement over the phone concerning the facts surrounding your accident. You should not provide a statement without first speaking with your attorney. The claims representative represents the responsible party, and does not represent your interests. The claims representative may attempt to get you to admit full or partial responsibility for the incident, or try to obtain a quick settlement at an amount well below the value of your claim.

In the months following your accident, your attorney will exchange correspondence and engage in settlement negotiations with the claims representative. During that time, all of your medical records will be provided to the insurance carrier, as well as documentation of lost wages, medical expenses and any other economic damages you may have suffered as a result of the accident. If a mutually agreeable settlement cannot be reached within a reasonable time period, formal legal action will likely be initiated.

RESPONDING TO A CLAIM AGAINST YOU

As a homeowner or business owner it is vital that you obtain liability insurance to cover you for accidents that occur on your property. A property owner may be held liable in many instances and would have to pay injury claims out of his or her own pocket if they did not carry an insurance liability policy.

For example, if you are a homeowner or business and there has been a recent snowfall, you are responsible for clearing the snow and ice off of your sidewalk within a reasonable amount of time following the precipitation so that pedestrians are able to walk on the sidewalk without the risk of falling. If someone does fall and sustain injuries, and you do not have liability insurance, you may be liable for that person's medical bills and related costs, lost wages, and pain and suffering award.

If you are a business owner, you likely maintain a liability insurance policy for protection against losses due to personal injuries sustained on the business premises. However, it is always more prudent and cost-effective to try and prevent accidents from occurring in the first place. Insurance companies recommend the loss prevention tips listed below to business owners to help reduce liability. Even if a claim is made, these efforts will weigh in the property owner's favor and may assist in preparing a successful defense.

1. Make a thorough inspection of the premises on a regular basis for unsafe conditions that could lead to a potential accident.

2. Keep floors clean and in good repair and make any necessary repairs immediately.

3. Keep aisles free and clear of fallen merchandise or foods. If there is a spill, post an appropriate warning sign and clean up the debris immediately.

4. Be particularly prudent during inclement whether. Devise a snow and ice removal plan and make sure all entrances have rugs to keep the floors dry.

5. Install non-slip flooring and use only non-slip wax on floor surfaces.

6. Repair damage to stairs, sidewalks and pavement as soon as possible, and place appropriate warning signs until the repairs are completed.

7. Make sure exterior lighting is adequate for both safety and security purposes.

8. Watch for hidden defects or dangerous conditions.

If, despite the preventive measures taken, an accident still occurs and someone is injured on your home or business property, you should promptly notify your insurance carrier. In fact, most insurance policies have a requirement that the insured notify the insurance company of any potential claim within a certain period of time after an incident occurs. Do not discuss the incident directly with the injured party or their representative. Refer all correspondence and phone calls to your insurance carrier or your lawyer.

It is also prudent to document the incident. For example, take photographs of the area immediately following the accident. Write down any statements made by the injured party. Record the facts so that you can refresh your memory when you are asked for a statement by your insurance claims representative and/or attorney.

If you have any information that would lead you to believe the claimant was responsible for their own injuries—e.g., because they were careless or intoxicated—you should obtain the names, addresses and telephone numbers of any witnesses who saw the accident and support your contentions.

You should also immediately remedy the condition that caused the accident in the first place, if in fact there was such a condition. The fact that an individual was injured on your property by whatever condition existed places you on notice. If another person injures themselves as a result of the same condition, it would be extremely difficult to defend that claim.

In general, the fact that a property owner takes steps to make repairs on an unsafe condition on their property following an accident cannot be used as evidence of liability because there is a public safety concern that property owners maintain their premises in a safe condition. If a property owner risked liability because they made their property safer, they would be less likely to make the repairs.

CHAPTER 3:
PREMISES LIABILITY LITIGATION

IN GENERAL

If your attorney is unable to settle your claim with the insurance carrier, it will be necessary to initiate formal litigation against the party responsible for your injuries. To begin litigation, the attorney will prepare a summons and complaint which details your claims and the basis of liability. For the purposes of litigation, the injured party is known as the "plaintiff" and the responsible party is known as the "defendant." The defendant is served with the complaint, and is required to serve his or her answer to the complaint within a prescribed period of time.

A sample Premises Liability Complaint is set forth at Appendix 2.

STATUTE OF LIMITATIONS

Every state has a statute of limitations which "limits" the time you have to bring legal action against the responsibility party. In general, most premises liability claims require that the plaintiff initiate formal legal action within 3 years from the date the claim accrued. The accrual date is typically the date the accident occurred and the injuries were sustained.

In addition, most statutes require you to give notice to governmental entities, such as municipalities, within as little as 30 to 90 days of the incident. If you do not give the required notice, or file a claim or lawsuit within the time set by law for the jurisdiction in which the injury occurred, you lose your ability to recover for your injuries.

Governmental immunity and the Notice of Claim requirement are discussed further in Chapter 6 of this almanac.

RESPONSIBLE PARTIES

In order to maintain a premises liability lawsuit, there must be a "responsible" party. For example, a person who trips and falls on the property of another is not automatically entitled to recover damages for his or her injuries. If an individual falls simply because he is not watching where he is going, he cannot recover no matter how severe the injuries may be, unless they are somehow connected to the negligence of another.

When a person is injured through no fault of his or her own, but due to the negligence of another, it must be determined which party is liable and subject to suit. Oftentimes, there are a number of persons or entities who may be held responsible in a premises liability case. For example, if a business rents space from the owner of the premises, both the building owner and the occupant of the space may be named as defendants. Thus, a party who is an owner or possessor of the property has a duty to use reasonable care with respect to the premises under its control, and to keep those premises in a safe condition for others. An owner or possessor may include a party which manages the premises.

For example, a landlord may be liable to the tenant or third parties for injuries caused by dangerous or defective conditions on the rental property. In order to hold the landlord responsible, however, the tenant must be able to prove that the landlord was negligent, and that the landlord's negligence caused an injury. The tenant must be able to show that:

1. The landlord had control over the problem that caused the injury;

2. The accident was foreseeable;

3. Repairing the problem would not have been unreasonably expensive or difficult;

4. A serious injury was the probable consequence of not fixing the problem;

5. The landlord failed to take reasonable steps to avoid the accident;

6. The landlord's failure to repair the problem caused the tenant's accident; and

7. The tenant was genuinely hurt as a result of the landlord's negligence.

For example, if a tenant falls and breaks his ankle on a broken step, the landlord will be liable if the tenant can show that:

1. It was the landlord's responsibility to maintain the staircase;

2. An accident of this type was foreseeable;

3. A repair would have been easy or inexpensive;

4. The probable result of a broken step is a serious injury;

5. The landlord failed to take reasonable measures to maintain the steps;

6. The broken step caused his injury; and

7. The victim sustained injuries as a result.

The injured person may file a premises liability lawsuit seeking damages for medical bills, lost earnings, pain and other physical suffering, permanent physical disability and disfigurement and emotional distress.

Liability for Independent Contractors

If a dangerous condition is created by a party, even though the party may not have control of or occupy the premises when the injury occurs, there still may be a duty of care. Thus, where a third party independent contractor is responsible for maintaining the premises, such as a floor cleaning company, or providing security on the premises, such as a private security service, they may also be named as a defendant.

For example, in Valenti v. NET Properties Management, Inc., 710 A.2d 399 (Sup. Ct., N.H., 1998), a shopping mall hired an independent contractor to design the mall's entryway, and another to maintain the entryway and mall floors. The plaintiff slipped and fell on the wet entryway, breaking her hip. She sued the shopping mall. The question presented to the court was whether the shopping mall or the independent contractors were actually liable for the plaintiff's injuries.

The court stated that, as a general rule, an employer is not liable for the negligence of its independent contractor. However, it went on to point out that there were many exceptions to that general rule. The Court cited Section 425 of the Restatement (Second) of Torts, which provides:

> One who employs an independent contractor to maintain in safe condition land which he holds open to the entry of the public as his place of business . . . is subject to the same liability for physical harm caused by the contractor's negligent failure to maintain the land . . . in reasonably safe condition, as though he had retained its maintenance in his own hands.

Thus, the Court held that the shopping mall could be subject to liability for the independent contractor's negligence and ruled that the plaintiff's lawsuit against the shopping mall could be maintained.

Public Sidewalks

A governmental entity may be liable for failure to maintain a public sidewalk in a safe condition. Some laws require the business owner to maintain the public sidewalk located directly adjacent to their property, however, if they fail to do so, the municipality is generally required to make the repairs and issue a citation to the negligent business owner. In such a case, it is always prudent to name both the municipality and the private business owner as co-defendants.

BURDEN OF PROOF

The plaintiff in a premises liability action has the burden of proving that the owner or possessor of the property was negligent—e.g., in the maintenance of the property—and thus breached some "duty" owed to the injured person, and that this breach of duty "caused" the plaintiff's injuries. These are the basic "elements" which support the cause of action and permit the plaintiff to maintain the lawsuit.

Duty and Status of Plaintiff

The duty owed by the owner or possessor of the property generally depends on the status of the plaintiff, i.e., the classification of the persons on the property as either licensees, invitees, or trespassers, as further set forth below. The distinction may lower, but never raise, the normal duty of reasonable care and, therefore, benefits owners generally. Licensees and invitees are owed a higher standard of care because they have permission to be on the premises. The lowest duty of care is owed to a trespasser. Once it has been established that there is a relationship between the parties in which a duty has arisen, it must be shown that the defendant breached that duty in some manner.

Licensees

A licensee is one who has permission or consent, either expressly or implied, to go on the premises of another merely for his own interests, convenience, or gratification. Under the common law, the owner or possessor of the land had no duty to inspect the land for unsafe conditions, or even to warn the licensee if there were known dangers on the property. The licensee had no right to request that the possessor of the property make the premises safe insofar as the licensee is generally present on the property for his or her own benefit.

Most jurisdictions now require that the owner or possessor of the property use reasonable care in maintaining the property in a safe condition for the licensee. Thus, an owner is subject to liability for physical harm caused to licensees by a condition on the property if:

1. The owner knew or had reason to know of the condition, should have realized it involved an unreasonable risk of harm to licensees, and should have expected that licensees would not discover the danger;

2. The owner failed to exercise reasonable care to make the condition safe or to warn licensees of the condition and risk; and

3. The licensees did not know or have reason to know of the conditions and the risk involved.

Invitees

An invitee is an individual who enters and remains on premises at the express or implied invitation of the person who owns or possesses the premises. Where an owner or possessor of land, by express or implied invitation, induces others to come upon his premises for any lawful purpose, he is liable in damages to such persons for injuries caused by his failure to exercise ordinary care in keeping the premises safe. The invitation may be express, implied from known and customary use of portions of the premises, or inferred from conduct actually known to the owner or his authorized agent.

Under the common law, the highest duty is owed to an invitee and is two-fold:

1. There is a duty to use reasonable care to maintain the premises in a safe condition and to take reasonable care in investigating the existence of any potentially unsafe conditions on the property; and

2. There is a duty to provide warnings to the invitee about any concealed dangers which are known to the premises owner but which may not be readily discernable by the invitee.

Obviously, the adequacy of safety measures taken depends on the type of premises. For example, in a supermarket, items are often dropped and broken in the aisles. There is a duty to be on the lookout for these types of spills and immediately clean the area because the floor could become slippery and dangerous to customers.

An owner is subject to liability for physical harm caused to invitees by a condition on the property if:

1. The owner knew or had reason to know of the condition and should have realized it involved an unreasonable risk of harm to invitees;

2. The owner should have expected that invitees would not have discovered or realized the dangers; and

3. The owner failed to exercise reasonable care to protect invitees from the danger.

If a party negligently creates a dangerous condition or circumstance, then that party has a duty to take action to prevent injury or damage if it is reasonable to foresee that others might be injured or damaged.

Trespassers

Under the common law, an owner is not liable to a trespasser for injuries caused by the owner's failure to exercise reasonable care to make the land safe. However, an owner who knows, or should know, that there are trespassers who constantly intrude on the property, is liable for bodily harm caused them by an unsafe condition on the property if:

1. The condition is one the owner created or maintained;

2. The condition is likely to cause death or serious bodily harm;

3. The condition is of such a nature that the owner has reason to believe that trespassers will not discover it; and

4. The owner has failed to exercise reasonable care to warn trespassers of the condition and risk involved.

For example, it has been held that where a property owner is aware that individuals use a portion of their premises as a shortcut, the owner has a duty to inspect the property for potentially dangerous conditions and undertake any repairs necessary to make the property safe. Thus, in cases where the danger is known to the owner and not known to the one injured, the property owner may be liable.

Attractive Nuisance

The concept of attractive nuisance arose to protect trespassing children in circumstances in which their presence could be reasonably anticipated on property where there is an unreasonable risk of injury. The basis for liability is the property owner's knowledge of the dangerous condition on the property.

The attractive nuisance doctrine is discussed more fully in Chapter 4 of this Almanac.

Knowledge of the Dangerous Condition

As it pertains to licensees and invitees, a crucial element of a premises liability case is demonstrating that the property was in a "dangerous condition" when the injury occurred, and the owner or possessor had knowledge of the dangerous condition. However, not every condition on a property that causes injury is a so-called "dangerous condition." In order to be deemed a dangerous condition, a premises defect must meet two conditions:

1. The premises must constitute an unreasonable risk to the licensee or invitee; and

2. The condition must have been one that the plaintiff should not have anticipated under the existing circumstances.

For example, it has been held that it is a matter of common knowledge that dirt becomes soft and muddy when wet. Therefore, the premises owner or possessor should not have to warn of, or make reasonably safe, such a condition which a reasonable and prudent person would have anticipated encountering on a rainy day.

Further, it has been held that in order to establish knowledge of the dangerous condition, the owner must have:

1. Created the condition;

2. Known the condition existed and negligently failed to alleviate the condition; or

3. The condition must have existed for such a length of time as to show that it should have been discovered and remedied.

Nevertheless, an owner or possessor's creation of a condition does not conclusively establish that he had "knowledge" that the condition was "dangerous." Proof that the owner or possessor of the property created a condition which posed an unreasonable risk of harm may infer negligence, or constitute circumstantial evidence that the owner or possessor knew of the condition, however, creating the condition does not establish "knowledge" as a matter of law for the purposes of establishing premises liability.

Foreseeability and Notice

In order for the owner or possessor to be deemed negligent, there is a common law requirement that it be foreseeable that his conduct created the danger. The risk of injury to the third party must have been foreseeable for the actor to be held responsible. If a reasonable prudent person could not have foreseen the probability that injury would occur as a result of his conduct, there is no negligence and no liability.

In Wal-Mart Stores, Inc. v. Gonzalez, 968 S.W.2d 934 (Sup. Ct., Tex., 1998), the plaintiff slipped and fell on some cooked macaroni salad in a Wal-Mart cafeteria. She sued and was awarded $100,000.

Wal-Mart appealed the verdict and the appellate court reversed the trial court's decision. Although the court recognized that the store owes invitees a duty to exercise reasonable care to protect them from dangerous conditions in the store that are known or discoverable to it, it held that the evidence showed that the plaintiff was the only person who saw the macaroni salad on the floor, and this was insufficient evidence to demonstrate that the store had constructive knowledge of the condition.

The Court further set forth the requirements which a plaintiff must prove to recover damages in a slip and fall case:

1. Actual or constructive knowledge of some condition on the premises by the owner/operator;

2. The condition posed an unreasonable risk of harm;

3. The owner/operator did not exercise reasonable care to reduce or eliminate the risk; and

4. The owner/operator's failure to use such care proximately caused the plaintiff's injuries.

Proximate Cause

In order to prove "causation," the plaintiff must establish that there was a direct connection between the negligence of the property owner and the injuries sustained by the plaintiff. If the plaintiff's injuries were caused by other factors, such as their own negligence, causation cannot be established.

The plaintiff must further prove that the foreseeable injury sustained as a result of the breach of duty was proximately caused by the negligent act or omission of the defendant. The act is a proximate cause of the injury if it was a substantial factor in bringing about the injury, and without which the result would not have occurred.

The tests used by the courts to determine whether proximate cause exists are the "but for" and the "substantial factor" test. The "but for" test asks the question: Would the injury not have occurred "but for" the negligence of the defendant? If the answer is yes, then proximate cause exists. The "substantial factor" test is used when the fact pattern is more complicated and there exists more than one cause for the plaintiff's injury. In that case, proximate cause exists for all of the acts or omissions which were substantial factors in bringing about the injury, and without which the injury would not have occurred.

Dangerous and Hazardous Condition

As set forth above, property owners and possessors are responsible for injuries that occur as a result of a dangerous or hazardous condition on their property, which they either knew about or should have known about. The hazard may be obvious or hidden, and may be permanent or temporary.

In general, an owner will be considered to have knowledge of a dangerous or hazardous condition if it is permanent in nature—e.g., a large crack in the pavement—since the owner knew, or should have known, about the condition before the incident occurs. If the condition is temporary—e.g., spilled liquid—the length of time that the condition existed before the incident occurred may be a determining factor in establishing the owner's knowledge. For example, if the spill occurred immediately prior to the accident, the property owner may not be liable since the owner could not have known about the spill before the accident occurred. However, if the spill was present for some period of time before the accident then the owner may be liable, even if the owner did not know about the spill before it occurred.

STATUTORY VIOLATIONS

In certain cases, the violation of a statute, ordinance or building code may be proof of a violation of the requisite standard of care in the civil case and creates a rebuttable presumption that the actor was negligent. The violation is known as "negligence per se." In determining whether the violation may be applied as proof of negligence, there are two questions which should be asked:

(1) Is the injured person within the class of persons who are protected by statute from suffering a certain injury? and

(2) Is the particular injury the statute seeks to prevent the same injury the plaintiff has suffered?

If the answer to both questions is yes, then the violation of that statute may be introduced as evidence of the wrongdoer's negligence.

For example, a building code may require the installation of child guards on all windows. If the landlord fails to comply with this requirement and, as a result, a young child falls from a window and is injured, the landlord's failure to install the child guard could be used as evidence of negligence. The two criteria set forth above have been met if:

1. The child is within the class of persons that were to be protected under the statute; and

2. The injuries sustained in a fall from the window are those types of injuries that the statute sought to prevent.

On the other hand, if the tenant removed the child guard, the landlord would be able to use that fact to defend himself against the claim.

The Uniform Building Code (UBC) developed by the International Congress of Building Officials is the most widely used model building code in the United States. There are also regional building codes—e.g., the BOCA National Building Code and the Southern Building Code—which address special requirements based on hazards that may occur in a particular region, e.g., floods, earthquakes, etc. An International Building Code is presently being developed to replace the Uniform, National and Southern Building Codes.

The reader is advised to check with the local building department to determine which of the model codes has been adopted in a particular jurisdiction. Copies of the building codes may be obtained from these local departments or from the region's building code sponsoring organization.

A Directory of Building Code Sponsors is set forth at Appendix 3.

RETAINING AN EXPERT

Many premises liability cases require the testimony of an expert witness where particular issues are beyond the common understanding of a jury. For instance, an expert might assist the jury in determining whether the property owner defendant complied with building codes, as discussed above. The expert will also evaluate the condition of the property where the accident occurred, and testify as to the cause of the fall, based on the expert's education, training, and experience.

Expert testimony may also be used to show design deficiencies, inadequacy of lighting, and negligence in maintenance and security procedures. In slip and fall cases, expert testimony may be required on the "coefficient of friction," which is a measure of the slipperiness of a floor. Factors that affect the coefficient of friction include substances on the floor, walking speed, slope of the floor, the type of shoe worn by the plaintiff, and anti-slip devices, such as abrasive strips.

Medical experts and economists are generally necessary to support damage claims, such as the extent and permanence of an injury, and future lost wages.

DAMAGES

Once it has been determined that there is liability, the question turns to whether damages were caused as a result of the negligence. In premises liability law, damages are usually measured in terms of monetary compensation. There are three basic categories of money damages recoverable in a premises liability case:

1. Compensatory damages;

2. Punitive damages, and

3. Nominal damages.

Compensatory Damages

Compensatory damages represent an attempt to compensate the injured party for the actual harm he suffered, by awarding the amount of money necessary to restore the plaintiff to his pre-injury condition. Often, a complete restoration cannot be accomplished. In such cases, damages also include the monetary value of the difference between the plaintiff's pre-injury and post-injury conditions. Most jurisdictions divide these damages into two general categories—economic and noneconomic.

The importance of categorizing damages as economic or noneconomic lies in the fact that noneconomic damages are often capped under state law. For example, in Kansas, noneconomic damages are capped in all personal injury cases at a maximum of $250,000, no matter how many defendants contributed to cause the injuries, and no matter how serious the injury. In contrast, Missouri has no caps on noneconomic damages in premises liability cases.

Economic Damages

Economic damages include almost everything that can be replaced with money. These losses are projected into the future based, among other factors, on medical testimony regarding continuing disability and future needs. This category of damages is very broad, varies from case to case, and can include:

Medical Expenses

The reasonable expenses of necessary medical care, hospitalization and treatment related to the defendant's wrongful conduct are recoverable. Medical expenses are the most concrete and objectively demonstrable items to identify.

Lost Earnings and Impairment of Earning Capacity

Lost earnings and impairment of earning capacity are the most justifiable element of a general compensatory damages award from a strictly economic point of view.

Necessary Services

A plaintiff may recover the reasonable value of services provided by family members for free, and the cost of hiring others to perform normal household duties, such as cleaning, shopping, etc.

Loss of Spousal Services

The spouse of the injured person may be able to recover the value of the injured person's services.

Damage to Personal Property

The rules in case of damage to personal property are simple and straightforward. The basic measure is the difference between the market value of the property before the injury and its market value after. If the property has been totally destroyed, the market value after the injury will be the salvage value, if any.

The cost of repairs are included, in addition to payment for devaluation, if any, after repair. The plaintiff may also be able to recover for the loss of use of the property while it is repaired or replaced, as long as it is within a reasonable time period.

Non-Economic Damages

Noneconomic damages are those losses which cannot be quantified in a dollar amount, such as pain and suffering, mental anguish, disfigurement, and loss of enjoyment of life. Pain and suffering is the most difficult element of recovery to measure. This is a broad concept, which may include a number of more or less separate factors, the most common of which is the physical pain associated with the injury. Recovery for mental suffering associated with bodily disfigurement is also includible as an element of pain and suffering.

Loss of enjoyment of life may relate to life in all of its aspects or merely in certain aspects. For example, if a plaintiff enjoyed playing piano as a hobby, and has suffered an injury to his hands, the plaintiff has suffered a loss of enjoyment in relation to the ability to play the piano. Of course, if this were the plaintiff's livelihood, the damages for loss of earning capacity would also be involved, and would greatly increase the measure of damages.

Punitive Damages

Punitive damages involve an award of a substantial amount of money to the plaintiff for the purpose of punishing the defendant. Ordinary negligence on the part of a property owner is not enough to allow a plaintiff to recover punitive damages. Most jurisdictions require proof of misconduct beyond ordinary negligence. This would usually mean proof that the defendant acted in a "wanton or intentional" way, which would include the "reckless disregard" of a known danger to the plaintiff's health and safety. In a premises liability case, it is often difficult to establish conduct on the part of the defendant sufficient to allow recovery of punitive damages.

The Issue of Fault

In assessing a damage claim, the issue of fault is of particular concern. If you are 100% innocent, then you are entitled to the full value of your claim. However, if you were partly to blame for the accident which resulted in your injuries, your culpability generally reduces your recovery proportionately according to the degree of your fault. For example, if your damage award is $100,000, and you are found 25% liable for the accident, your recovery would be reduced to $75,000.

On the other hand, if you were mostly at fault for the accident, your recovery would be reduced considerably and, depending on the jurisdiction, may even be eliminated entirely.

CHAPTER 4:
SPECIAL CONSIDERATIONS

IN GENERAL

As set forth below, special care must be taken when considering premises safety for children and the elderly.

THE ELDERLY

Scope of the Problem

According to the National Center for Injury Prevention and Control (NCIPC), falls are the leading cause of injury deaths among people 65 years and older in the United States, and one of every three Americans 65 years old or older falls each year.

For adults 65 years old or older, 60% of fatal falls happen at home, 30% occur in public places, and 10% occur in health care institutions. According to the National Safety Council (NSC), more than 86 percent of those people sustaining fatal injuries due to falls in the home were 65 years old or older. In addition, people over 65 years of age suffer from one-half of the fatalities due to injuries sustained in public places.

Among older adults, falls are the most common cause of injuries and hospital admissions for trauma. Advanced age greatly increases the chance of a hospital admission following a fall. Falls are also the second leading cause of spinal cord and brain injury among older adults, and account for 87% of all fractures for people 65 years and older. The most common are fractures of the pelvis, hip, femur, vertebrae, humerus, hand, forearm, leg and ankle.

Of all fractures from falls, hip fractures cause the greatest number of deaths and lead to the most severe health problems in the elderly population. In 1996, there were approximately 340,000 hospital admissions for hip fractures in the United States. Most patients with hip fractures are hospitalized for about 2 weeks, and one-half of all older adults hospitalized for hip fractures cannot return home or live independently after their injuries. People who are 85 years or older are 10-15 times more likely to experience hip fractures than are people between the ages of 60 and 65, and women sustain 75%–80% of all hip fractures.

The costs for fall-related injuries among the elderly population are staggering. Direct costs include out-of-pocket expenses and charges paid by insurance companies for the treatment of fall-related injuries. These include costs and fees associated with hospital and nursing home care, physician and other professional services, rehabilitation, community-based services, the use of medical equipment, prescription drugs, local rehabilitation, home modifications, and insurance administration. This does not account for the long term consequences of these injuries, such as disability, decreased productivity, or quality of life.

According to the NCIPC, in 1994, the average direct cost for a fall injury was $1,400 for a person over the age of 65, and the total direct cost of all fall injuries for people age 65 and older in 1994 was $20.2 billion. By 2020, the cost of fall injuries is expected to reach $32.4 billion.

Contributory Factors

There are a number of factors that contribute to the high incidence of falling among the elderly, including gait and balance problems, dementia, vision problems, neurological and/or musculoskeletal problems, and the use of medication. Environmental hazards such as slippery surfaces, uneven floors, poor lighting, loose rugs, unstable furniture, and objects on floors only exacerbate the problem.

Given the above facts, it is no surprise that many premises liability claims involve falls by elderly people. That is why it is crucial, particularly for a business owner whose clientele consist of elderly patrons, to be particularly vigilant when inspecting their property for potentially unsafe conditions. The avoidance of fall injuries by careful planning and preventive measures is essential, however, it is inevitable that some falls will still occur. Potholes, uneven sidewalks and curbs, debris left in aisles, slippery stairs, are all potentially lethal for the elderly population.

In fact, staircases are particularly dangerous for elderly people, who account for 85 percent of all stairway fall fatalities. Step overhangs catch the foot if the elderly person is unable to raise their foot high enough when climbing the stairs. Property owners should inspect the staircases, paying particular attention to the carpets used on stairs, the tread depth and spacing, and other design aspects of staircases to make sure they do not propose an unnecessary danger to elderly patrons.

Litigation

Although a senior citizen's pre-existing problems may contribute to his or her accident, and may make it difficult for an attorney to establish causation, where there is negligence on the part of the property owner, a claim should nonetheless be pursued. Even if the award is relatively small, making a claim will bring the unsafe condition to the attention of the property owner. On the other hand, if a claim is never made, the unsafe condition would likely remain until the next victim is injured.

It is the very threat of being sued that will most likely bring about a change. The attorney representing the injured party will argue that the fall would not have occurred had the property owner designed the premises with the safety of all patrons in mind. The jury will hear the evidence and decide whether the property owner was negligent and, if so, award damages.

As set forth in Chapter 2, a finding of negligence requires the plaintiff to show that the defendant (i) owed a duty of care toward the plaintiff; (ii) breached that duty; (iii) that the breach of duty proximately caused the injury; and (iv) that the plaintiff suffered damage as a result.

The elderly plaintiff's biggest problem in meeting the burden of proof is causation and the multiple factors which may contribute to an elderly person's fall. The defense is certain to put forth these alternative theories of causation and impeach the plaintiff's claim that the negligence of the defendant was to blame for the fall.

In addition, the defense has the advantage that, by the time the case reaches trial, the memories of the plaintiff may have faded considerably. Therefore, it is important that the elderly plaintiff's deposition be performed early in the discovery phase so that his or her statements are preserved when the memory of the event is still relatively fresh in his or her mind.

Nursing Homes

More than 1.5 million elderly people live in nursing homes today and, as the elderly population increases, so will the nursing home population. As further discussed below, the duty of a nursing home is to use reasonable care in light of the known physical and mental condition of the elderly resident. Since the elderly residents of nursing homes have unique characteristics, there also arises a special duty owed by the nursing home.

Falls

It is common for an elderly resident to sustain a fall in a nursing home. Although the elderly are entitled to a higher duty of care from those responsible for their care, the duty of care by the caregiver is not absolute. For example, constant individual supervision is not required. The defense will likely argue that they complied with the state's regulations and thus were not negligent. However, minimum compliance will not absolutely negate negligence.

In establishing negligence, the plaintiff must show that the defendant deviated from the applicable standard of care. In this case, the standard is that of reasonable care, considering the patient's known mental and physical condition. For example, if an elderly person is known to wander away from the premises, failure to maintain adequate supervision may result in a finding of negligence if that patient wanders off and sustains injuries.

In addition, in considering the elderly resident's physical or mental impairments, a contributory negligence claim by the defense may be excused. For example, if the floor was recently mopped and a warning sign is placed at the site, but the resident, because of failing vision, is unable to read the sign and falls, the defense may not be able to assert contributory negligence where the resident's condition was known to the caregiver.

In support of this proposition, courts have held that a person who suffers from impaired senses and mental faculties due to old age is not guilty of contributory negligence where his failure to use that degree of care which an ordinary prudent person would use under the same or similar circumstances is due to such disability.

Therefore, it is important to carefully examine the resident's daily living and medical records, interview witnesses, and depose the caregivers, to establish their awareness of the elderly resident's physical and mental limitations.

Building Codes

Federal, state and local building and fire codes have been enacted to help establish safety standards in buildings. For example, a smoke detector and/or sprinkler requirement in a nursing home may mean the difference between life and death, particularly for an elderly person who likely needs more time to exit the premises.

Local building codes that govern a residential, skilled care, or recreational facility for elders are generally adapted from one of the three model building codes discussed in Chapter 3. Whether or not a facility violated a building code depends on what code was adapted for that particular area. For example, the smoke detector requirement varies among jurisdictions. The National Building Code, followed in northeastern and midwestern states, and the Uniform Fire Code, followed in western states, require smoke detectors in patient rooms whereas the Southern Building Code does not have the same requirement.

Thus, it is important to check all applicable building and fire codes when investigating a premises liability claim arising in the context of a nursing home or other residential facility designed for an elderly population. The safety standards in federally assisted facilities are governed by the U.S. Department of Housing and Urban Development (HUD), and should also be examined where applicable.

CHILDREN

Like the elderly, children are another segment of the population who are particularly susceptible to unintentional injury and death, and who are therefore owed a special duty of care.

Attractive Nuisance

An attractive nuisance is something on a property that is potentially harmful, and so inviting or interesting to a child that it would lure the child onto the property to play with it or explore the area. A common example of an attractive nuisance is an unenclosed swimming pool which would be very inviting to a young child who is unaware of the extent of the danger.

As set forth in Chapter 1, property owners have a special legal responsibility to try to prevent injuries to children who may wander onto the property even though the child is technically a "trespasser" on the premises. According to the Restatement of Torts, a property owner or possessor is liable for an injury to trespassing children if:

1. The place where the condition is maintained is one where the owner knows or should know that young children are likely to trespass;

2. The condition is one which the possessor knows, or should know, and which he realizes or should realize involves an unreasonable risk of death or serious bodily harm to such children;

3. The children, because of their youth, do not discover the condition or realize the risk involved in coming within the area made dangerous by it; and

4. The utility to the possessor of maintaining the condition is slight as compared to the risk to young children who trespass thereon.

Nevertheless, a dangerous condition on the property is not necessarily an attractive nuisance. For example, a natural lake or rocky cliff may be dangerous, however, they are not considered attractive nuisances because the property owner did not create or maintain them. In addition, the age of the child would be taken into consideration in determining the extent to which they should have realized the danger.

Therefore, property owners should regularly inspect their property to see whether there are any potentially dangerous conditions that might attract children. If so, they should take immediate action to rectify the unsafe condition. In addition, property owners should be aware of any local building code requirements that govern.

For example, because of the high incidence of drowning deaths among young children, most jurisdictions have regulations concerning swimming pools. Commonly, a swimming pool is required to be enclosed in a fence on all four sides. The fence must be a certain height—e.g., 4 feet—and cannot have openings which would allow a young child to climb over the fence. In addition, the enclosure must generally have a self-closing, self-latching gate with the placement of the latch at a certain height so that a small child cannot open it. If the property owner does not comply with these regulations, and a child is injured as a result, the owner may be held strictly liable for those injuries.

Falls

According to the National Center for Injury Prevention and Control (NCIPC), falls are the leading cause of non-fatal unintentional injuries and emergency department visits for children between 0 and 14-years-old, and each year this group accounts for an estimated 2.5 million emergency room visits.

One of the most common places for a child to sustain injuries as a result of a fall is on a playground. According to the NCIPC, each year in the United States, 200,000 preschool and elementary school children visit emergency rooms for injuries sustained on playground equipment. In 1995, the costs of playground-related injuries were $1.2 billion for children younger than 15 years old.

A nationwide investigation of public playgrounds by the Public Interest Research Groups (PIRG) and Consumer Federation of America (CFA) found that a majority of American playgrounds pose hidden threats to children. Some of the documented hazards existing in playgrounds include inadequate protective surfacing; obstacles in the "fall zone" of climbing equipment; excessive heights on play equipment; close proximity of swings; improperly sized openings in play equipment allowing for a child's head to get lodged in the opening; dangerous play equipment; and protrusions from play equipment, e.g., bolts.

If a child is injured in a fall, particularly on a playground which is purportedly designed and intended for active play, one must carefully investigate the situs of the accident to determine whether there exists a hazardous condition which should have been corrected.

Lead-Based Paint

As set forth in Chapter 1, lead poisoning in children caused by lead-based paint is a serious health-related environmental hazard for children. The Residential Lead-Based Paint Hazard Reduction Act, commonly known as Title X, was enacted in 1992 to address this serious problem. The Environmental Protection Agency (EPA) is responsible for promulgating the regulations implementing Title X, which applies to rental property built before 1978.

Under Title X, a landlord is required to give a prospective tenant a pamphlet prepared by the EPA entitled "Protect Your Family From Lead In Your Home" prior to signing a lease. Both the landlord and tenant must also sign an EPA-approved disclosure form stating that the landlord advised the tenants of any known lead paint conditions in the home. The disclosure form must be kept on file by the landlord for approximately three years.

If the landlord fails to comply with Title X, they could be liable to the tenants in a premises liability action for any injuries which were causally-related to the lead-based paint. Under Title X, the landlord faces penalties of up to $10,000 for each violation. Further, if a tenant is injured by the owner's willful non-compliance, the landlord could be assessed with treble damages.

Additional information on Title X and lead poisoning is available from the National Lead Clearinghouse by calling (800) 424-LEAD, or from the Office of Lead Hazard Control at their internet website: http://www.hud.gov/lea/leahome.html.

The following properties are not covered by Title X:

1. Housing certified as lead-free by an accredited lead inspector;

2. Lofts, efficiencies and studio apartments;

3. Short-term vacation rentals;

4. A single room rented in a residential dwelling;

5. Retirement communities—i.e., housing designed for seniors where one or more tenants is at least 62 years old—unless children are present.

CHAPTER 5:
THE PREMISES SECURITY CLAIM

IN GENERAL

A rapidly growing area of premises liability involves criminal acts by third persons. The law states that one who maintains control over the safety and security of the premises owes a duty to use reasonable care to protect tenants against unreasonable and foreseeable risks of harm from the criminal acts of third parties.

For example, landlords are generally responsible for keeping the rental property safe and secure for tenants and guests—e.g., making sure that doors and windows have proper locks and common areas are well-lit, etc. Most states hold landlords legally responsible to some degree in protecting their tenants from burglars and other criminals, as well as from the criminal actions of co-tenants and employees.

The failure to make a reasonable assessment of the crime potential of the area, and follow up with security measures designed to eliminate or reduce the threat of safety, may subject the landlord to a greater degree of legal liability if a tenant is injured as a result of the landlord's negligence.

Landlords must also be vigilant about tenant crime. For example, the landlord may be held legally responsible for tenants who deal drugs from their apartments, particularly if it can be shown that the landlord was aware of the situation and failed to take any action against the tenant. For this reason, landlords must be particularly careful during the tenant screening process, be aware of activities taking place on the rental property, and take swift action if a problem arises.

Landlords should also be careful when hiring employees, such as a superintendent or building manager, because such employees generally have access to the individual rentals. A thorough background check should be undertaken prior to hiring. If a building employee causes injury or property loss to a tenant, the landlord will generally be held liable under the legal doctrine of "respondeat superior," which states that the employer is liable for the acts of the employees.

ELEMENTS

In a premises security case, the plaintiff must demonstrate why the property owner is responsible for the injuries suffered by the crime victim—i.e., that the injuries were the result of the owner's negligence. In general, the following elements must be met:

Duty

Business Invitee

The owner or possessor of premises is liable to business invitees for crime committed by third parties. According to Section 324A of the Restatement (Second) of Torts:

> One who undertakes, gratuitously or for consideration, to render services to another which he should recognize as necessary for the protection of a third person or his things, is subject to liability to the third person or his things, for physical harm resulting from his failure to exercise reasonable care to protect his undertaking, if
>
> (a) his failure to exercise reasonable care increases the risk of such harm, or
>
> (b) he has undertaken to perform a duty owed by the other to the third person, or
>
> (c) the harm is suffered because of reliance of the other or the third person upon the undertaking.

Landlord/Tenant

A landlord has a recognized duty to use due care to make common premises safe, as against foreseeable risks. The duty owed to the tenant is also owed to an invitee of the tenant and extends to the portions of the premises the landlord retains in his control.

The elements of the existence of a landlord-tenant relationship are:

1. A contract, express or implied, between the parties;

2. The creation of an estate in the tenant, either at will or for a specified term;

3. Reversion to the landlord; and

4. The transfer of exclusive possession and control to the tenant.

According to Section 360 of the Restatement (Second) of Torts:

> A possessor of land who leases a part thereof and retains in his own control any other part which the lessee is entitled to use as appurtenant to the part leased to him, is subject to liability to his lessee and others lawfully upon the land with the consent of the lessee or a sublessee for physical harm caused by a dangerous condition upon that part of the land retained in the lessor's control.

Breach of Duty

Business Invitee

Once duty has been established, the frequency and nature of the crimes occurring on or near the premises, whether violent or not, are relevant for the jury to assess the level of care required to protect the invitee's person and property. In order to establish negligence, the plaintiff must show that the owner failed to use "ordinary care" to reduce or eliminate an unreasonable risk of harm which was known or should have been known to the owner, and which was created by the condition of the property.

Landlord/Tenant

The landlord-tenant relationship gives rise to potential liability which does not arise in normal business invitee cases. A tenant, and his or her invitees, enjoys a greater degree of protection over a business invitee. Thus, when a tenant is injured on a portion of the landlord's premises over which the landlord has retained control, a duty to protect is imposed as a matter of law. Once the legal duty has been established, a plaintiff must ordinarily show that a defendant failed to exercise due care to make common areas reasonably safe against foreseeable risks.

For example, if a tenant is assaulted by a criminal who was able to gain access to the rental property because the landlord failed to repair a broken lock on the front door of the apartment building, the landlord may have breached his duty to protect the tenant.

Joint and Several Liability

Where two or more property owners owe a duty to business invitees, they are subject to joint and several liability in a negligence action by a crime victim.

In Merrill Crossings Assoc. v. McDonald, 705 So.2d 560 (Sup. Ct., Fla., 1998), the Florida Supreme Court held that negligence by retail store owners in providing adequate security to protect their patrons in a common parking lot resulted in a criminal attack and thus subjected them to joint and several liability.

The defendants argued that they should not be held liable because the criminal assault on the plaintiff was an intervening act. However, the Court held that it would be irrational to allow a party who negligently fails to provide reasonable security measures to reduce its liability because there is an intervening intentional tort, where the intervening intentional tort is exactly what the security measures were supposed to protect.

Proximate Cause

To establish that negligence was a proximate cause of the injury suffered, plaintiff must show that the injury would not have occurred but for the defendant's negligence.

For example, in Ramos v. 1199 Housing Corporation, 678 NYS2d 110 (2d Dept. 1998), the plaintiffs were unable to prevail in a lawsuit against the landlord and its security guard company because there was no evidence produced as to who the assailant was nor how he gained access to the building. Thus, there was no proof that the landlord was in any way negligent in allowing the criminal to enter the building.

In another case, Liller v. Quick Stop Food Mart, Inc., 507 S.E.2d 602 (Ct. App., N.C., 1998), the Court dismissed the plaintiff's claim that the convenience store where he was shot by an assailant should have had more security. The Court held that the store's failure to have more security was not the proximate cause of the assault on the plaintiff insofar as the assailant was irrational—allegedly drunk or high on drugs—and thus would not have been deterred by ordinary security precautions.

Foreseeability

Foreseeability is a crucial element in a premises security case. The standard of proof is that a property owner may be liable for criminal acts committed against a person on his or her property if he knew or had reason to know that a criminal attack was likely. The plaintiff must generally demonstrate that the property owner could foresee that the type of injury which occurred could occur and did not take adequate security measures to prevent the injury.

Evidence of prior crimes is generally critical to successfully prosecuting a premises security claim. The plaintiff may have to establish that there had been a significant amount of criminal activity on or near the premises that would put a reasonable property owner on notice that security measures were warranted.

For example, if a number of apartment break-ins have been reported in a certain neighborhood, and a building owner fails to provide adequate locks on the front door of the building, the owner may be liable to an individual who is the victim of such a break-in.

The duty to protect invitees and licensees from criminal acts of third parties extends to premises which are adjacent to public walkways if the criminal contact is foreseeable. This would include the sidewalk at the front of a store or other business. However, it has been held that there is no duty where there is an occurrence off of the premises completely.

For example, in Gonzalez v. South Dallas Club, 951 S.W.2d 72 (Tex. 1997), following a bar fight, the participants left the premises and continued the fight at another location approximately one mile from the bar. The bar owner was sued. The plaintiff alleged that because the initial fight took place on the premises of the bar, coupled with the fact that liquor had been consumed at the bar, criminal contact was foreseeable, therefore the defendant owed a duty to protect against criminal actions. The Corpus Christi Court of Appeals noted that the defendant did not control the location where the assault actually occurred and, therefore, there was no duty on the part of the defendant bar owner to provide any type of security at the second location.

Because foreseeability is a major factor in establishing liability, there is no duty and, therefore, no liability without first establishing that there was a foreseeable risk of harm from criminal acts of third persons.

The Restatement (Second) of Torts sets forth a two-part test to determine foreseeability in premises security cases:

1. Specifically, did the owner realize, or should he have realized, the likelihood that such acts were occurring or about to occur?; and

2. Generally, did the owner know or have reason to know from past experience of a likelihood of conduct on the part of a third person which would endanger the safety of invitees?

In Boone v. Martinez, 567 N.W.2d 508 (Sup. Ct., Minn., 1997), the plaintiff—who had previously been beaten up by the assailant—sued the bar for negligent failure to exercise reasonable care to control and secure its patrons and premises. The Minnesota Supreme Court reversed the lower court decision, and held that a sudden, vicious attack of a bar patron by another patron does not constitute the element of causation under a negligence claim against the bar owners. The Court further stated that in order to establish an innkeeper's liability, a plaintiff must prove the following four elements:

1. The proprietor must be put on notice of the offending party's vicious or dangerous propensities by some act or threat,

2. The proprietor must have an adequate opportunity to protect the injured patron,

3. The proprietor must fail to take reasonable steps to protect the injured patron, and

4. The injury must be foreseeable.

Insofar as the evidence established that the assault was sudden and unforeseeable, without warning, and lasted no more than 3 minutes, the Court held that there was insufficient evidence to allow the jury to decide if the bar was aware of the defendant's vicious or dangerous propensities.

CASE INVESTIGATION

In investigating a premises security case, one must first establish the status of the victim on the premises. For example, was the victim legally on the premises, e.g., a tenant or business invitee. As set forth in Chapter 2, this status carries with it a higher duty of care than would be owed a trespasser.

Have the victim prepare a chronology of the events. Obtain the names and addresses of witnesses, if any, and conduct interviews with them. Pay particular attention to statements which would support your contention that the property owner was negligent. For example, a fellow tenant may know how long a dangerous condition on the premises was permitted to remain, such as a broken lock. You may find that there have been written or verbal reports to the landlord concerning the condition.

If a police report was filed, obtain a copy and carefully analyze the facts. If the criminal was apprehended, conduct a background investigation to determine whether he has a criminal record, particularly for similar type crimes. Also determine where the criminal's prior offenses took place. In large complexes, it may be that the criminal lived in the building. If so, liability may attach if the landlord did not make a sufficient inquiry into the background of the individual when renting the apartment. Investigate the rate of crime in the area where the incident occurred. If there is a history of recurring crime on or near the premises, and the owner failed to take any measures to safeguard the premises, the owner's failure to address the problem will support a negligence claim.

CAMPUS SECURITY

The Jeanne Clery Disclosure of Campus Security Policy and Campus Crime Statistics Act

The "Jeanne Clery Disclosure of Campus Security Policy and Campus Crime Statistics Act" (originally known as the "Campus Security Act") was enacted by the United States Congress and signed into law by President George Bush in 1990. The Act, codified at 20 USC 1092 (f) as a part of the Higher Education Act of 1965, is a federal law that requires colleges and universities to disclose certain timely and annual information about campus crime and basic security policies. The law was re-named in 1998 in memory of Jeanne Clery, a 19-year old freshman who was murdered at Lehigh University in 1986.

The Act governs all public and private institutions of postsecondary education participating in federal student aid programs. Under the Act, schools are required to publish an annual report each year by October 1st. The report must detail 3 year's worth of campus crime statistics and detail certain security policy statements, including (i) the school's sexual assault policies; (ii) the law enforcement authority of campus police; and (iii) the procedure by which students report crimes.

The report is to be made available automatically to all current students and employees. Prospective students and employees are to be given an opportunity to request a copy of the report. The report can be placed on the school's website provided the school notifies all persons entitled to a copy as to the internet address, and where paper copies can be obtained if desired.

Violators of the Act can be "fined" up to $25,000 by the U.S. Department of Education or face other enforcement action.

Crime Statistics

As set forth above, the report must disclose crime statistics for the campus, unobstructed public areas immediately adjacent to or running through the campus, and certain non-campus facilities. For the purposes of disclosure, off-campus fraternity and sorority houses are considered part of the campus as long as they are officially recognized by the institution.

The statistics must be gathered from campus police or security, local law enforcement, and other school officials. Crimes are to be reported in the following categories:

1. Criminal Homicide

   (a) Murder and Nonnegligent Manslaughter

    (b) Negligent manslaughter

  2. Sex Offenses

    (a) Forcible Sex Offenses

    (b) Nonforcible Sex Offenses

  3. Robbery

  4. Aggravated Assault

  5. Burglary

  6. Motor Vehicle Theft

  7. Arson

Schools are also required to report the following three types of incidents if they result in either an arrest or disciplinary referral:

  1. Liquor Law Violations

  2. Drug Law Violations

  3. Illegal Weapons Possession

The statistics are also broken down geographically into "on campus," "residential facilities for students on campus," noncampus buildings, or "on public property" such as streets and sidewalks.

Timely Information

Schools are also required to provide "timely warnings" and a separate more extensive "public crime log." The timely warning requirement is triggered when the school considers a crime to pose an ongoing "threat to students and employees" while the public crime log records all incidents reported to the campus police or security department.

Timely warnings cover a broader source of reports than the crime log but are limited to those crime categories required in the annual report. The crime log includes only incidents reported to the campus police or security department, but covers all crimes—not just those required in the annual report. The log must be publicly available during normal business hours, and remain open for 60 days.

The text of the Act is set forth at Appendix 4.

CHAPTER 6:
GOVERNMENTAL IMMUNITY

IN GENERAL

Under the common law, governmental entities enjoy full sovereign immunity. The concept of sovereign immunity consists of two basic principles of law:

1. The state as sovereign is immune from suit without consent even though there is no dispute regarding the state's liability; and

2. The state has immunity from liability even though the state has consented to be sued.

Thus, any plaintiff bringing a suit for money damages against a governmental entity has the burden of proving the state has waived both immunity from suit and liability.

Unlimited governmental immunity is less common in modern times, largely because government has expanded so much over the last century. The federal government as well as a majority of states have adopted legislation which limits the sovereign immunity of government. Although the legislation varies from state to state, the underlying principles are basically the same, and many of the states have modeled their legislation after the Federal Tort Claims Act.

THE FEDERAL TORT CLAIMS ACT (28 U.S.C. § 1346)

Prior to 1946, the federal government could not be sued for property damage, personal injury, or wrongful death caused by its employees unless there was some Act of Congress that specifically provided relief in limited circumstances. After many years of debate, Congress finally enacted the Federal Tort Claims Act ("FTCA") in 1946.

The FTCA allows individuals to recover from the federal government for property damage, personal injury, and wrongful death caused by the negligence of a federal employee. Since the Act was passed, Americans have recovered millions of dollars from the United States for the negligent acts of its employees.

Under the FTCA, individuals may recover for numerous types of injuries, including but not limited to, those suffered in slips and falls in government facilities. Generally, the injury must be the result of the negligence of a federal employee who was in the performance of their job.

Under the FTCA, the government can only be sued under circumstances where the United States, if a private person, would be liable to the claimant in accordance with the law of the place where the act or omission occurred. Thus, the Act does not apply to conduct that is uniquely governmental, i.e, incapable of being performed by a private individual.

Choice of Law

Federal law governs the procedure for processing claims against the United States. State law generally governs the type of injuries for which, and the amount of damages that, an individual may recover. The Act specifies that the liability of the federal government is to be determined in accordance with the law of the place where the act or omission occurred. In an action under the FTCA, a court must apply the law the state courts would apply in the analogous tort action, including federal law.

Covered Federal Employees

Covered federal employees under the Federal Tort Claims Act include:

1. Officers or employees of any Federal agency;

2. Persons acting in official capacity;

3. Employees temporarily or permanently in service of the United States, with or without compensation,

4. Civil Air Patrol, if under Air Force direction and control, or

5. Air National Guard if in Federal status.

Employees Acting Within Scope of Employment

For the Act to apply, the employee must have been acting within the scope of his or her employment. The legal determination of whether an employee is acting within the scope of his or her employment is made according to local law after reviewing all relevant facts and circumstances.

Ordinarily, a person is acting within the scope of employment if his or her actions were directed, expressly or impliedly, by competent authority and were serving at least in part a governmental purpose, when the negligent act or omission allegedly occurred.

The substitution provision of the Federal Employees Liability Reform and Tort Compensation Act (FELRTCA) provides that the United States shall be substituted as the party defendant for a employee acting within the scope of his office or employment at the time of the incident out of which the claim arose. The purpose of this amendment was to remove the potential personal liability of Federal employees for common law torts committed within the scope of their employment, and provide that the exclusive remedy for such torts is through an action against the United States under the Federal Tort Claims Act.

Independent Contractors

Under the Federal Tort Claims Act, the U.S. is subject to liability for the negligence of an independent contractor only if it can be shown that the government had authority to control the detailed physical performance of the contractor and exercised substantial supervision over its day-to-day activities.

Time Limitation

The statute of limitations under the Federal Tort Claims Act requires that an individual make their claim against the federal government, in writing, within two (2) years after their claim accrues. A claim generally "accrues" at the time of injury when essential facts are apparent. However, under limited circumstances, a claim may not be deemed to have accrued until the claimant knew, or should have known, of the existence of the negligent act.

The claim is a prerequisite to filing a lawsuit against the United States. Although a limited exception may apply, an individual who believes that they have been injured by the negligence of a federal employee should not delay in making their claim to avoid having their claim dismissed should the exception be deemed not to apply in their case.

THE CLAIM

In order to recover under the Federal Tort Claims Act, the claim must be for money damages in a specific amount. There is no other relief available under the Act.

The claim must allege that there has been:

1. Damage to real property or personal property;

2. Personal injury; or

3. Death.

The claim must also allege that there has been a negligent or wrongful act or omission by a federal employee. A negligent act means that the person has departed from the conduct expected of a reasonably prudent person under similar circumstances.

Claims Excluded

Under the Federal Tort Claims Act, the government is not liable when any of its employees or agents commits the torts of assault, battery, false imprisonment, false arrest, malicious prosecution, abuse of process, libel, slander, misrepresentation, deceit, or interference with contract rights except for:

1. Those claims arising out of medical, dental or health care functions, or

2. Those claims arising out of acts or omissions of investigative or law enforcement officers.

Law Enforcement Officers

If a law enforcement officer commits assault, battery, false imprisonment, false arrest, abuse of process, or malicious prosecution, the government has limited its immunity. However, the government is not liable if the claim against the law enforcement officers is for libel, slander, misrepresentation, deceit, or interference with contract.

Additional claims specifically excluded by the Act include, but are not limited to:

1. Damages, injuries, or death that stem from the performance of or failure to perform a discretionary function by a federal agency or government employee. Absent specific statutes or regulations, where the particular conduct is discretionary, the failure of the government properly to train its employees who engage in that conduct is also discretionary;

2. Admiralty claims—i.e., claims that occur on navigable waters and are payable by other means;

3. Intentional torts—i.e., acts that the person intends to commit;

4. Claims arising in a foreign country;

5. Claims alleging a government "taking" of air space over land;

6. Claims arising from damage to property of United States Government departments or agencies;

7. Claims for personal injury, death or property damage incurred "incident to service" by a member of the Armed Forces or Air National Guard; and

8. Claims for personal injury or death incurred "in performance of duty" by a civilian employee of United States.

Selected provisions of the Federal Tort Claims Act are set forth at Appendix 5.

STATE GOVERNMENT IMMUNITY STATUTES

As set forth above, many states have modeled their own governmental immunity statutes after the Federal Tort Claims Act. For example, Texas enacted a Tort Claims Act which created a limited waiver of sovereign immunity for certain torts. Prior to enactment of the Texas Tort Claims Act, sovereign immunity precluded suit and liability in tort against the state, counties, and municipalities carrying out governmental functions. Governmental entities were not liable for torts committed by their officers or agents. Therefore, they could not be held liable under either an agency or respondeat superior theory of liability for the acts of their employees, agents, and officers.

Under the Texas Tort Claims Act, the legislature waived immunity both from suit and liability for the claims authorized in the legislation. Nevertheless, governmental entities continue to enjoy complete immunity both from suit and liability for claims not specifically waived by statute. Thus, as stated above, plaintiffs bringing a tort claim against a governmental entity bear the burden of establishing either that their claim falls within the Texas Tort Claims Act or some other waiver of sovereign immunity.

Under the Texas Tort Claims Act, a governmental unit in the state is liable for personal injury and death caused by a "condition or use" of tangible personal or real property if the governmental unit would, were it a private person, be liable to the claimant according to Texas law.

However, the statute further specifically defines and limits governmental liability for "premises defects," stating that: "If a claim arises from a premise defect, the governmental unit owes to the claimant only the duty that a private person owes to a licensee on private property, unless the claimant pays for the use of the premises."

Thus, while the Texas Tort Claims Act initially grants a very broad waiver of immunity, the waiver of immunity and extent of liability are very limited in premises defect cases, and does not create a cause of action measured by an ordinary care standard. This provision is typical of most state requirements under which the government may be liable for negligent acts which result in a dangerous "condition" on government property but enjoy more limited liability for a "premises defect."

Premises Defect

A plaintiff injured by a premises defect on government property is generally limited to bringing a premises liability claim as provided for in the government's immunity statute. If the government limits its liability for premises defects, the plaintiff may not deprive the government of that limited liability by taking the position that a premises defect is a negligent "use of property" for which the government may have waived its immunity. Thus, a plaintiff who prevails at trial upon a negligence standard may have that judgment reversed on appeal if it is determined that the claim actually arose from a premises defect.

Nevertheless, a finding that a case is a premises defect claim does not necessarily dispose of the determination of the applicable standard of liability. For example, under the Texas Tort Claims Act, there are five different standards of care:

1. The duty owed to a licensee in the event of a dangerous condition;

2. The duty not to injure a licensee through gross negligence;

3. The duty owed to invitees in the case of a "special defect";

4. The duty in the case of a malfunctioning traffic signal or control device; and

5. The duty owed to a person who pays for the use of the premises.

At common law, the duty owed to the plaintiff was determined by the plaintiff's status on the premises, as discussed in Chapter 2. However, the common law tests for determining the status of an injured party in a premises liability case are irrelevant in a suit under the Texas Tort Claims Act. In that case, as set forth above, the duty owed to a plaintiff is determined by the type of premise defect at issue and whether the plaintiff paid for the use of the premises.

Special Defects

A "special defect" is generally something out of the ordinary course of events rather than a long-standard, routing, or permanent defect—i.e., a dangerous condition of such magnitude that it places a higher duty of care on the government, such as a roadway obstruction or excavation. Courts have construed "special defects" to include those defects that present an unexpected and unusual danger to ordinary users of roadways. To constitute a special defect, the condition must also be of such a character and location that it endangers ordinary users of a highway, road, or street. A factor to be considered in determining whether a special defect exists is the size of the dangerous condition.

Texas case law has established five principles to consider in determining whether a condition on a property constitutes a special defect:

1. Most property defects are ordinary premises defects not special defects. Thus, a special defect is the exception and not the rule.

2. A special defect need not have been created by the governmental unit itself, but could conceivably result from a natural occurrence such as an obstruction created by an avalanche or from the act of a third party;

3. To constitute a special defect, the defect must be of such a size that a person cannot drive down the roadway without having to encounter it.

4. The defect must present an unexpected and unusual danger to ordinary users of roadways.

5. In order to be found to be a special defect the premises condition must be on a highway, road, or street.

In general, a "special defect" eliminates the requirement of actual knowledge before the government is obligated to act. In the case of a special defect, the plaintiff obtains the status of an invitee. Consequently, the government occupant has an ordinary care duty to warn of dangerous conditions of which the government has knowledge or which the government would have discovered in the exercise of ordinary care.

PRIOR WRITTEN NOTICE REQUIREMENT

Most municipalities, as a condition precedent to a liability lawsuit, require that the municipality have actual written notice of the street or sidewalk defect which caused the accident. The required notice may be in the form of a written notification of the defect, filed with the appropriate governmental agency, or from a prior notice of claim which relates to the same defect. Generally, if the municipality does not have any prior written notice of the defect, the claim will be dismissed.

For example, in Sylvester v. Chicago Park District, 698 N.E.2d 1119 (Sup. Ct., Ill., 1998), a patron of the City of Chicago football stadium suffered injuries from tripping over a concrete block placed on a dimly lit walkway in the City of Chicago parking lot. She subsequently brought a negligence lawsuit to recover damages for her injuries.

Although the City of Chicago admitted the concrete car stop was in an improper location, it presented an affirmative defense—i.e., that it was not liable for the negligence alleged because the public property was used for recreational purposes.

Reversing the judgments of the trial and appellate courts, the Illinois Supreme Court held that the City was entitled to immunity. The parking lot is an extension of Soldier Field, so it is part of a city recreation facility. The Illinois Tort Immunity Act provides that a local public entity shall not be liable for injury occurring on public property unless it is proven that the local public entity has . . . notice of the injury causing condition. Under the facts, the plaintiff could not prove that the City of Chicago had notice of the dangerous condition, thus, the court held that it could not be held liable in negligence.

NOTICE OF CLAIM REQUIREMENT

Most government immunity statutes require that the governmental entity receive prompt notice of the plaintiff's claim. Such notice is generally a prerequisite to the bringing of a lawsuit. The time period within which the governmental unit must have actual or formal notice of the accident giving rise to the lawsuit is generally set forth in the statute, e.g., 90 days or 180 days.

The notice requirement is intended to insure that the governmental unit has an opportunity to investigate the accident while the facts are still relatively recent, enabling them to settle the case or prepare its defense. Accordingly, a formal notice must notify the defendant of the injury, and the time, manner, and place of the incident giving rise to the claim. Generally, if the plaintiff does not serve a formal notice on the governmental unit within the prescribed time period, he or she is precluded from bringing a lawsuit. The time for giving notice generally begins on the date of the incident.

A sample Notice of Claim is set forth at Appendix 6.

APPENDIX 1:
SAMPLE ATTORNEY RETAINER AGREEMENT IN A PREMISES LIABILITY ACTION

RETAINER AGREEMENT

DATED this 14th day of February, 2000, the undersigned, JOHN DOE, ("Client"), residing at 100 First Street, New York, New York 10002, retains and employs MARGARET C. JASPER ("Attorney") as his attorney to represent him with full authorization to do all things necessary to investigate and prosecute his claims against XYZ SUPERMARKET, located at 1 Main Street, New York, New York 10001, relating to personal injuries sustained as a result of a fall which occurred on or about December 30, 1999.

The undersigned agrees to the following terms and conditions:

1. Attorney has agreed to take client's case on a contingency fee basis. This means that attorney's legal fees will be paid only if client receives a monetary judgment or settlement in this matter. Attorney will receive no fee if there is no recovery. The contingency fee in this matter will be one-third of any amount recovered by settlement or judgment. In addition, it may be necessary for Attorney to advance certain expenses during the course of litigation. Such expenses, if any, to the extent they are not prepaid by Client, shall be subtracted from any sum recovered after the attorney fee is deducted. If no recovery is made, Client will not be responsible for any attorney fee whatsoever.

2. Client understands and agrees that Attorney cannot commence work in this matter until this agreement is signed and returned to attorney's office.

3. Attorney agrees not to enter into any settlement agreement without the consent of Client.

4. Attorney acknowledges that a payment in the amount of $_____ towards expenses accompanies this retainer agreement.

5. By signing below where indicated, Client acknowledges that he has received a copy of this retainer letter and has read and agreed to its terms and conditions.

ACCEPTED BY: _____

John Doe, Client

The above employment is hereby accepted on the terms stated.

ACCEPTED BY: _____

Margaret C. Jasper, Attorney

APPENDIX 2:
SAMPLE PREMISES LIABILITY COMPLAINT

[NAME OF COURT]

[CAPTION OF CASE] [FILE INDEX NUMBER]

COMPLAINT

Plaintiff, by his attorney, [name of attorney], complaining of the defendant, alleges, as follows:

FIRST: Upon information and belief at all times hereinafter mentioned the defendant was and still is a domestic corporation, duly organized and existing under and by virtue of the laws of the State of New York.

SECOND: Upon information and belief at all times hereinafter mentioned the defendant owned a supermarket located at 1 Main Street, New York, New York 10001, in the Borough of Manhattan, City and State of New York.

THIRD: Upon information and belief, at all times hereinafter mentioned the defendant managed, operated, maintained and controlled those premises.

FOURTH: That the public, and more particularly, the plaintiff, were invited to the premises of the defendant for the purpose of purchasing various grocery items from the defendant.

FIFTH: That on the 27th day of March, 2000, the plaintiff, while lawfully on the above premises, was caused to fall, due to the negligence of the defendant, its agents, servants and/or employees.

SIXTH: That the defendant, its agents, servants and/or employees were negligent in that they failed to clean a slippery substance from the floor of an aisle in the premises and failed to warn the public, and more particularly, the plaintiff, of the dangerous condition existing on the premises, and in generally being careless and reckless concerning the hazardous condition on the premises.

SEVENTH: Upon information and belief at that time and place defendant had actual knowledge and notice of the dangerous condition existing on the premises or the condition had existed for a sufficient length of time prior to the accident such that the defendant could and should have had such knowledge and notice.

EIGHTH: That the accident and resulting injuries were due to the negligence of the defendant, its agents, servants and/or employees.

NINTH: That as a result of the negligence of the defendant the plaintiff was rendered sick, sore, lame and disabled and suffered serious and painful injuries in and about his head, body and limbs, and has been informed and believes that he will continue to suffer therefrom for an indefinite period of time in the future and that such injuries may be permanent in nature.

TENTH: That by the reason of the negligence of the defendant, the plaintiff has been damaged in the sum of One Hundred Thousand ($100,000) Dollars.

WHEREFORE, plaintiff demands judgment against defendant in the amount of One Hundred Thousand Dollars ($100,000); costs and disbursements of this action; and any other relief the Court deems appropriate.

PLEASE TAKE NOTICE, that pursuant to the CPLR, you are required to serve a copy of your answer within 20 days after the service of this Complaint.

Dated:

[Signature Line]

[Name of Attorney]

Attorney for Plaintiff

[Attorney's Address]

[Attorney's Telephone Number]

APPENDIX 3:
DIRECTORY OF BUILDING CODE
SPONSORS

ORGANIZATION	ADDRESS	TELEPHONE NUMBER
Building Officials and Code Administrators International (BOCA)	4051 West Flossmoor Road Country Club Hills, IL 60578	708-799-2300/ 800-323-1103
International Conference of Building Officials (ICBO)	5360 South Workman Mill Road Whittier, CA 90611	310-699-0541
Southern Building Code Congress International (SBCCI)	900 Montclair Road Birmingham, AL 35213	205-591-1853/ 800-877-2224
Council of American Building Officials (CABO)	5203 Leesburg Pike, Suite 708 Falls Church, VA 22041	703-931-4533

APPENDIX 4:
THE JEANNE CLERY DISCLOSURE OF CAMPUS SECURITY POLICY AND CAMPUS CRIME STATISTICS ACT (20 USC § 092(F))

20 U.S.C. §1092

(f) Disclosure of campus security policy and campus crime statistics

(1) Each eligible institution participating in any program under this subchapter and part C of subchapter I of chapter 34 of Title 42 shall on August 1, 1991, begin to collect the following information with respect to campus crime statistics and campus security policies of that institution, and beginning September 1, 1992, and each year thereafter, prepare, publish, and distribute, through appropriate publications or mailings, to all current students and employees, and to any applicant for enrollment or employment upon request, an annual security report containing at least the following information with respect to the campus security policies and campus crime statistics of that institution:

(A) A statement of current campus policies regarding procedures and facilities for students and others to report criminal actions or other emergencies occurring on campus and policies concerning the institution's response to such reports.

(B) A statement of current policies concerning security and access to campus facilities, including campus residences, and security considerations used in the maintenance of campus facilities.

(C) A statement of current policies concerning campus law enforcement, including—

(i) the enforcement authority of security personnel, including their working relationship with State and local police agencies; and

(ii) policies which encourage accurate and prompt reporting of all crimes to the campus police and the appropriate police agencies.

(D) A description of the type and frequency of programs designed to inform students and employees about campus security procedures and practices and to encourage students and employees to be responsible for their own security and the security of others.

(E) A description of programs designed to inform students and employees about the prevention of crimes.

(F) Statistics concerning the occurrence on campus, in or on noncampus buildings or property, and on public property during the most recent calendar year, and during the 2 preceding calendar years for which data are available—

(i) of the following criminal offenses reported to campus security authorities or local police agencies:

(I) murder;

(II) sex offenses, forcible or nonforcible;

(III) robbery;

(IV) aggravated assault;

(V) burglary;

(VI) motor vehicle theft;

(VII) manslaughter;

(VIII) arson; and

(IX) arrests or persons referred for campus disciplinary action for liquor law violations, drug-related violations, and weapons possession; and

(ii) of the crimes described in subclauses (I) through (VIII) of clause (i), and other crimes involving bodily injury to any person in which the victim is intentionally selected because of the actual or perceived race, gender, religion, sexual orientation, ethnicity, or disability of the victim that are reported to campus security authorities or local police agencies, which data shall be collected and reported according to category of prejudice.

(G) A statement of policy concerning the monitoring and recording through local police agencies of criminal activity at off-campus student organizations which are recognized by the institution and that are engaged in by students attending the institution, including those student organizations with off- campus housing facilities.

(H) A statement of policy regarding the possession, use, and sale of alcoholic beverages and enforcement of State underage drinking laws and a statement of policy regarding the possession, use, and sale of illegal drugs and enforcement of Federal and State drug laws and a description of any drug or alcohol abuse education programs as required under section 1011(i) of this title.

(I) Redesignated (H)

(2) Nothing in this subsection shall be construed to authorize the Secretary to require particular policies, procedures, or practices by institutions of higher education with respect to campus crimes or campus security.

(3) Each institution participating in any program under this subchapter and part C of subchapter I of chapter 34 of Title 42 shall make timely reports to the campus community on crimes considered to be a threat to other students and employees described in paragraph (1)(F) that are reported to campus security or local law police agencies. Such reports shall be provided to students and employees in a manner that is timely and that will aid in the prevention of similar occurrences.

(4)(A) Each institution participating in any program under this subchapter [20 U.S.C.A. § 1070 et seq.] and part C of subchapter I of chapter 34 of Title 42 [42 U.S.C.A. § 2751 et seq.] that maintains a police or security department of any kind shall make, keep, and maintain a daily log, written in a form that can be easily understood, recording all crimes reported to such police or security department, including—

(i) the nature, date, time, and general location of each crime; and

(ii) the disposition of the complaint, if known.

(4)(B)(i) All entries that are required pursuant to this paragraph shall, except where disclosure of such information is prohibited by law or such disclosure would jeopardize the confidentiality of the victim, be open to public inspection within two business days of the initial report being made to the department or a campus security authority.

(4)(B)(ii) If new information about an entry into a log becomes available to a police or security department, then the new information shall be recorded in the log not later than two business days after the information becomes available to the police or security department.

(4)(B)(iii) If there is clear and convincing evidence that the release of such information would jeopardize an ongoing criminal investigation or the safety of an individual, cause a suspect to flee or evade detection, or result in the destruction of evidence, such information may be withheld until that damage is no longer likely to occur from the release of such information.

(5) On an annual basis, each institution participating in any program under this subchapter and part C of subchapter I of chapter 34 of Title 42 [42 U.S.C.A. § 2751 et seq.] shall submit to the Secretary a copy of the statistics required to be made available under paragraph (1)(F). The Secretary shall—

(A) review such statistics and report to the Committee on Education and the Workforce of the House of Representatives and the Committee on Labor and Human Resources of the Senate on campus crime statistics by September 1, 2000;

(B) make copies of the statistics submitted to the Secretary available to the public; and

(C) in coordination with representatives of institutions of higher education, identify exemplary campus security policies, procedures, and practices and disseminate information concerning those policies, procedures, and practices that have proven effective in the reduction of campus crime.

(6)(A) In this subsection:

(i) The term "campus" means—

(I) any building or property owned or controlled by an institution of higher education within the same reasonably contiguous geographic area of the institution and used by the institution in direct support of, or in a manner related to, the institution's educational purposes, including residence halls; and

(II) property within the same reasonably contiguous geographic area of the institution that is owned by the institution but controlled by another person, is used by students, and supports institutional purposes (such as a food or other retail vendor).

(ii) The term "noncampus building or property" means—

(I) any building or property owned or controlled by a student organization recognized by the institution; and

(II) any building or property (other than a branch campus) owned or controlled by an institution of higher education that is used in direct support of, or in relation to, the institution's educational purposes, is used by students, and is not within the same reasonably contiguous geographic area of the institution.

(iii) The term "public property" means all public property that is within the same reasonably contiguous geographic area of the institution, such as a sidewalk, a street, other thoroughfare, or parking facility, and is adjacent to a facility owned or controlled by the institution if the facility is used by the institution in direct support of, or in a manner related to the institution's educational purposes.

(6)(B) In cases where branch campuses of an institution of higher education, schools within an institution of higher education, or administrative divisions within an institution are not within a reasonably contiguous geographic area, such entities shall be considered separate campuses for purposes of the reporting requirements of this section.

(7) The statistics described in paragraph (1)(F) shall be compiled in accordance with the definitions used in the uniform crime reporting system of the Department of Justice, Federal Bureau of Investigation, and the modifications in such definitions as implemented pursuant to the Hate Crime Statistics Act. Such statistics shall not identify victims of crimes or persons accused of crimes.

(8)(A) Each institution of higher education participating in any program under this subchapter and part C of subchapter I of chapter 34 of Title 42 shall develop and distribute as part of the report described in paragraph (1) a statement of policy regarding—

(i) such institution's campus sexual assault programs, which shall be aimed at prevention of sex offenses; and

(ii) the procedures followed once a sex offense has occurred.

(8)(B) The policy described in subparagraph (A) shall address the following areas:

(i) Education programs to promote the awareness of rape, acquaintance rape, and other sex offenses.

(ii) Possible sanctions to be imposed following the final determination of an on-campus disciplinary procedure regarding rape, acquaintance rape, or other sex offenses, forcible or nonforcible.

(iii) Procedures students should follow if a sex offense occurs, including who should be contacted, the importance of preserving evidence as may be necessary to the proof of criminal sexual assault, and to whom the alleged offense should be reported.

(iv) Procedures for on-campus disciplinary action in cases of alleged sexual assault, which shall include a clear statement that—

(I) the accuser and the accused are entitled to the same opportunities to have others present during a campus disciplinary proceeding; and

(II) both the accuser and the accused shall be informed of the outcome of any campus disciplinary proceeding brought alleging a sexual assault.

(v) Informing students of their options to notify proper law enforcement authorities, including on-campus and local police, and the option to be assisted by campus authorities in notifying such authorities, if the student so chooses.

(vi) Notification of students of existing counseling, mental health or student services for victims of sexual assault, both on campus and in the community.

(vii) Notification of students of options for, and available assistance in, changing academic and living situations after an alleged sexual assault incident, if so requested by the victim and if such changes are reasonably available.

(8)(C) Nothing in this paragraph shall be construed to confer a private right of action upon any person to enforce the provisions of this paragraph.

(9) The Secretary shall provide technical assistance in complying with the provisions of this section to an institution of higher education who requests such assistance.

(10) Nothing in this section shall be construed to require the reporting or disclosure of privileged information.

(11) The Secretary shall report to the appropriate committees of Congress each institution of higher education that the Secretary determines is not in compliance with the reporting requirements of this subsection.

(12) For purposes of reporting the statistics with respect to crimes described in paragraph (1)(F), an institution of higher education shall distinguish, by means of separate categories, any criminal offenses that occur—

(A) on campus;

(B) in or on a noncampus building or property;

(C) on public property; and

(D) in dormitories or other residential facilities for students on campus.

(13) Upon a determination pursuant to section 1094(c)(3)(B) of this title that an institution of higher education has substantially misrepresented the number, location, or nature of the crimes required to be reported under this subsection, the Secretary shall impose a civil penalty upon the institution in the same amount and pursuant to the same procedures as a civil penalty is imposed under section 1094(c)(3)(B) of this title.

(14)(A) Nothing in this subsection may be construed to—

(i) create a cause of action against any institution of higher education or any employee of such an institution for any civil liability; or

(ii) establish any standard of care.

(14)(B) Notwithstanding any other provision of law, evidence regarding compliance or noncompliance with this subsection shall not be admissible as evidence in any proceeding of any court, agency, board, or other entity, except with respect to an action to enforce this subsection.

(15) This subsection may be cited as the "Jeanne Clery Disclosure of Campus Security Policy and Campus Crime Statistics Act".

APPENDIX 5:
SELECTED PROVISIONS OF THE FEDERAL TORT CLAIMS ACT AS AMENDED

Sec. 1346. United States as defendant

(a) The district courts shall have original jurisdiction, concurrent with the United States Court of Federal Claims, of:

(a)(1) Any civil action against the United States for the recovery of any internal-revenue tax alleged to have been erroneously or illegally assessed or collected, or any penalty claimed to have been collected without authority or any sum alleged to have been excessive or in any manner wrongfully collected under the internal-revenue laws;

(a)(2) Any other civil action or claim against the United States, not exceeding $10,000 in amount, founded either upon the Constitution, or any Act of Congress, or any regulation of an executive department, or upon any express or implied contract with the United States, or for liquidated or unliquidated damages in cases not sounding in tort, except that the district courts shall not have jurisdiction of any civil action or claim against the United States founded upon any express or implied contract with the United States or for liquidated or unliquidated damages in cases not sounding in tort which are subject to sections 8(g)(1) and 10(a)(1) of the Contract Disputes Act of 1978. For the purpose of this paragraph, an express or implied contract with the Army and Air Force Exchange Service, Navy Exchanges, Marine Corps Exchanges, Coast Guard Exchanges, or Exchange Councils of the National Aeronautics and Space Administration shall be considered an express or implied contract with the United States.

(b)(1) Subject to the provisions of chapter 171 of this title, the district courts, together with the United States District Court for the District of the Canal Zone and the District Court of the Virgin Islands, shall have exclusive jurisdiction of civil actions on claims against the United States, for money damages, accruing on and after January 1, 1945, for injury or loss of property, or personal injury or death caused by the negligent or wrongful act or omission of any employee of the Government while acting within the scope of his office or employment, under circumstances where the United States, if a private person, would be liable to the claimant in accordance with the law of the place where the act or omission occurred.

(b)(2) No person convicted of a felony who is incarcerated while awaiting sentencing or while serving a sentence may bring a civil action against the United States or an agency, officer, or employee of the Government, for mental or emotional injury suffered while in custody without a prior showing of physical injury.

(c) The jurisdiction conferred by this section includes jurisdiction of any set-off, counterclaim, or other claim or demand whatever on the part of the United States against any plaintiff commencing an action under this section.

(d) The district courts shall not have jurisdiction under this section of any civil action or claim for a pension.

(e) The district courts shall have original jurisdiction of any civil action against the United States provided in section 6226, 6228(a), 7426, or 7428 (in the case of the United States district court for the District of Columbia) or section 7429 of the Internal Revenue Code of 1986.

(f) The district courts shall have exclusive original jurisdiction of civil actions under section 2409a to quiet title to an estate or interest in real property in which an interest is claimed by the United States.

(g) Subject to the provisions of chapter 179, the district courts of the United States shall have exclusive jurisdiction over any civil action commenced under section 453(2) of title 3, by a covered employee under chapter 5 of such title.

Sec. 1402. United States as defendant

(a) Any civil action in a district court against the United States under subsection (a) of section 1346 of this title may be prosecuted only:

(a)(1) Except as provided in paragraph (2), in the judicial district where the plaintiff resides;

(a)(2) In the case of a civil action by a corporation under paragraph (1) of subsection (a) of section 1346, in the judicial district in which is located the principal place of business or principal office or agency of the corporation; or if it has no principal place of business or principal office or agency in any judicial district (A) in the judicial district in which is located the office to which was made the return of the tax in respect of which the claim is made, or (B) if no return was made, in the judicial district in which lies the District of Columbia. Notwithstanding the foregoing provisions of this paragraph a district court, for the convenience of the parties and witnesses, in the interest of justice, may transfer any such action to any other district or division.

(b) Any civil action on a tort claim against the United States under subsection (b) of section 1346 of this title may be prosecuted only in the judicial district where the plaintiff resides or wherein the act or omission complained of occurred.

(c) Any civil action against the United States under subsection (e) of section 1346 of this title may be prosecuted only in the judicial district where the property is situated at the time of levy, or if no levy is made, in the judicial district in which the event occurred which gave rise to the cause of action.

(d) Any civil action under section 2409a to quiet title to an estate or interest in real property in which an interest is claimed by the United States shall be brought in the district court of the district where the property is located or, if located in different districts, in any of such districts.

Sec. 1491. Claims against United States generally; actions involving Tennessee Valley Authority

(a)(1) The United States Court of Federal Claims shall have jurisdiction to render judgment upon any claim against the United States founded either upon the Constitution, or any Act of Congress or any regulation of an executive department, or upon any express or implied contract with the United States, or for liquidated or unliquidated damages in cases not sounding in tort. For the purpose of this paragraph, an express or implied contract with the Army and Air Force Exchange Service, Navy Exchanges, Marine Corps Exchanges, Coast Guard Exchanges, or Exchange Councils of the National Aeronautics and Space Administration shall be considered an express or implied contract with the United States.

(a)(2) To provide an entire remedy and to complete the relief afforded by the judgment, the court may, as an incident of and collateral to any such judgment, issue orders directing restoration to office or position, placement in appropriate duty or retirement status, and correction of applicable records, and such orders may be issued to any appropriate official of the United States. In any case within its jurisdiction, the court shall have the power to remand appropriate matters to any administrative or executive body or official with such direction as it may deem proper and just. The Court of Federal Claims shall have jurisdiction to render judgment upon any claim by or against, or dispute with, a contractor arising under section 10(a)(1) of the Contract Disputes Act of 1978, including a dispute concerning termination of a contract, rights in tangible or intangible property, compliance with cost accounting standards, and other nonmonetary disputes on which a decision of the contracting officer has been issued under section 6 of that Act.

(b)(1) Both the United States Court of Federal Claims and the district courts of the United States shall have jurisdiction to render judgment on an action by an interested party objecting to a solicitation by a Federal agency for bids or proposals for a proposed contract or to a proposed award or the award of a contract or any alleged violation of statute or regulation in connection with a procurement or a proposed procurement. Both the United States Court of Federal Claims and the district courts of the United States shall have jurisdiction to entertain such an action without regard to whether suit is instituted before or after the contract is awarded.

(b)(2) To afford relief in such an action, the courts may award any relief that the court considers proper, including declaratory and injunctive relief except that any monetary relief shall be limited to bid preparation and proposal costs.

(b)(3) In exercising jurisdiction under this subsection, the courts shall give due regard to the interests of national defense and national security and the need for expeditious resolution of the action.

(b)(4) In any action under this subsection, the courts shall review the agency's decision pursuant to the standards set forth in section 706 of title 5.

(c) Nothing herein shall be construed to give the United States Court of Federal Claims jurisdiction of any civil action within the exclusive jurisdiction of the Court of International Trade, or of any action against, or founded on conduct of, the Tennessee Valley Authority, or to amend or modify the provisions of the Tennessee Valley Authority Act of 1933 with respect to actions by or against the Authority.

Sec. 2401. Time for commencing action against United States

(a) Except as provided by the Contract Disputes Act of 1978, every civil action commenced against the United States shall be barred unless the complaint is filed within six years after the right of action first accrues. The action of any person under legal disability or beyond the seas at the time the claim accrues may be commenced within three years after the disability ceases.

(b) A tort claim against the United States shall be forever barred unless it is presented in writing to the appropriate Federal agency within two years after such claim accrues or unless action is begun within six months after the date of mailing, by certified or registered mail, of notice of final denial of the claim by the agency to which it was presented.

Sec. 2412. Costs and fees

(a)(1) Except as otherwise specifically provided by statute, a judgment for costs, as enumerated in section 1920 of this title, but not including the fees and expenses of attorneys, may be awarded to the prevailing party in any civil action brought by or against the United States or any agency or any official of the United States acting in his or her official capacity in any court having jurisdiction of such action. A judgment for costs when taxed against the United States shall, in an amount established by statute, court rule, or order, be limited to reimbursing in whole or in part the prevailing party for the costs incurred by such party in the litigation.

(a)(2) A judgment for costs, when awarded in favor of the United States in an action brought by the United States, may include an amount equal to the filing fee prescribed under section 1914(a) of this title. The preceding sentence shall not be construed as requiring the United States to pay any filing fee.

(b) Unless expressly prohibited by statute, a court may award reasonable fees and expenses of attorneys, in addition to the costs which may be awarded pursuant to subsection (a), to the prevailing party in any civil action brought by or against the United States or any agency or any official of the United States acting in his or her official capacity in any court having jurisdiction of such action. The United States shall be liable for such fees and expenses to the same extent that any other party would be liable under the common law or under the terms of any statute which specifically provides for such an award.

(c)(1) Any judgment against the United States or any agency and any official of the United States acting in his or her official capacity for costs pursuant to subsection (a) shall be paid as provided in sections 2414 and 2517 of this title and shall be in addition to any relief provided in the judgment.

(c)(2) Any judgment against the United States or any agency and any official of the United States acting in his or her official capacity for fees and expenses of attorneys pursuant to subsection (b) shall be paid as provided in sections 2414 and 2517 of this title, except that if the basis for the award is a finding that the United States acted in bad faith, then the award shall be paid by any agency found to have acted in bad faith and shall be in addition to any relief provided in the judgment.

(d)(1)

(A) Except as otherwise specifically provided by statute, a court shall award to a prevailing party other than the United States fees and other expenses, in addition to any costs awarded pursuant to subsection (a), incurred by that party in any civil action (other than cases sounding in tort), including proceedings for judicial review of agency action, brought by or against the United States in any court having jurisdiction of that action, unless the court finds that the position of the United States was substantially justified or that special circumstances make an award unjust.

(B) A party seeking an award of fees and other expenses shall, within thirty days of final judgment in the action, submit to the court an application for fees and other expenses which shows that the party is a prevailing party and is eligible to receive an award under this subsection, and the amount sought, including an itemized statement from any attorney or expert witness representing or appearing in behalf of the party stating the actual time expended and the rate at which fees and other expenses were computed. The party shall also allege that the position of the United States was not substantially justified. Whether or not the position of the United States was substantially justified shall be determined on the basis of the record (including the record with respect to the action or failure to act by the agency upon which the civil action is based) which is made in the civil action for which fees and other expenses are sought.

(C) The court, in its discretion, may reduce the amount to be awarded pursuant to this subsection, or deny an award, to the extent that the prevailing party during the course of the proceedings engaged in conduct which unduly and unreasonably protracted the final resolution of the matter in controversy.

(D) If, in a civil action brought by the United States or a proceeding for judicial review of an adversary adjudication described in section 504(a)(4) of title 5, the demand by the United States is substantially in excess of the judgment finally obtained by the United States and is unreasonable when compared with such judgment, under the facts and circumstances of the case, the court shall award to the party the fees and other expenses related to defending against the excessive demand, unless the party has committed a willful violation of law or otherwise acted in bad faith, or special circumstances make an award unjust. Fees and expenses awarded under this subparagraph shall be paid only as a consequence of appropriations provided in advance.

(d)(2) For the purposes of this subsection—

(A) "fees and other expenses" includes the reasonable expenses of expert witnesses, the reasonable cost of any study, analysis, engineering report, test, or project which is found by the court to be necessary for the preparation of the party's case, and reasonable attorney fees (The amount of fees awarded under this subsection shall be based upon prevailing market rates for the kind and quality of the services furnished, except that

(i) no expert witness shall be compensated at a rate in excess of the highest rate of compensation for expert witnesses paid by the United States; and

(ii) attorney fees shall not be awarded in excess of $125 per hour unless the court determines that an increase in the cost of living or a special factor, such as the limited availability of qualified attorneys for the proceedings involved, justifies a higher fee.);

(B) "party" means (i) an individual whose net worth did not exceed $2,000,000 at the time the civil action was filed, or (ii) any owner of an unincorporated business, or any partnership, corporation, association, unit of local government, or organization, the net worth of which did not exceed $7,000,000 at the time the civil action was filed, and which had not more than 500 employees at the time the civil action was filed; except that an organization described in section 501(c)(3) of the Internal Revenue Code of 1986 (26 U.S.C. 501(c)(3)) exempt from taxation under section 501(a) of such Code, or a cooperative association as defined in section 15(a) of the Agricultural Marketing Act (12 U.S.C. 1141j(a)), may be a party regardless of the net worth of such organization or cooperative association or for purposes of subsection (d)(1)(D), a small entity as defined in section 601 of title 5;

(C) "United States" includes any agency and any official of the United States acting in his or her official capacity;

(D) "position of the United States" means, in addition to the position taken by the United States in the civil action, the action or failure to act by the agency upon which the civil action is based; except that fees and expenses may not be awarded to a party for any portion of the litigation in which the party has unreasonably protracted the proceedings;

(E) "civil action brought by or against the United States" includes an appeal by a party, other than the United States, from a decision of a contracting officer rendered pursuant to a disputes clause in a contract with the Government or pursuant to the Contract Disputes Act of 1978;

(F) "court" includes the United States Court of Federal Claims and the United States Court of Appeals for Veterans Claims;

(G) "final judgment" means a judgment that is final and not appealable, and includes an order of settlement;

(H) "prevailing party", in the case of eminent domain proceedings, means a party who obtains a final judgment (other than by settlement), exclusive of interest, the amount of which is at least as close to the highest valuation of the property involved that is attested to at trial on behalf of the property owner as it is to the highest valuation of the property involved that is attested to at trial on behalf of the Government; and

(I) "demand" means the express demand of the United States which led to the adversary adjudication, but shall not include a recitation of the maximum statutory penalty (i) in the complaint, or (ii) elsewhere when accompanied by an express demand for a lesser amount.

(d)(3) In awarding fees and other expenses under this subsection to a prevailing party in any action for judicial review of an adversary adjudication, as defined in subsection (b)(1)(C) of section 504 of title 5, United States Code, or an adversary adjudication subject to the Contract Disputes Act of 1978, the court shall include in that award fees and other expenses to the same extent authorized in subsection (a) of such section, unless the court finds that during such adversary adjudication the position of the United States was substantially justified, or that special circumstances make an award unjust.

(d)(4) Fees and other expenses awarded under this subsection to a party shall be paid by any agency over which the party prevails from any funds made available to the agency by appropriation or otherwise.

(e) The provisions of this section shall not apply to any costs, fees, and other expenses in connection with any proceeding to which section 7430 of the Internal Revenue Code of 1986 applies (determined without regard to subsections (b) and (f) of such section). Nothing in the preceding sentence shall prevent the awarding under subsection (a) of section 2412 of title 28, United States Code, of costs enumerated in section 1920 of such title (as in effect on October 1, 1981).

(f) If the United States appeals an award of costs or fees and other expenses made against the United States under this section and the award is affirmed in whole or in part, interest shall be paid on the amount of the award as affirmed. Such interest shall be computed at the rate determined under section 1961(a) of this title, and shall run from the date of the award through the day before the date of the mandate of affirmance.

Sec. 2671. Definitions

As used in this chapter and sections 1346(b) and 2401(b) of this title, the term "Federal agency" includes the executive departments, the judicial and legislative branches, the military departments, independent establishments of the United States, and corporations primarily acting as instrumentalities or agencies of the United States, but does not include any contractor with the United States.

"Employee of the government" includes officers or employees of any federal agency, members of the military or naval forces of the United States, members of the National Guard while engaged in training or duty under section 316, 502, 503, 504, or 505 of title 32, and persons acting on behalf of a federal agency in an official capacity, temporarily or permanently in the service of the United States, whether with or without compensation.

"Acting within the scope of his office or employment", in the case of a member of the military or naval forces of the United States or a member of the National Guard as defined in section 101(3) of title 32, means acting in line of duty.

Sec. 2672. Administrative adjustment of claims

The head of each Federal agency or his designee, in accordance with regulations prescribed by the Attorney General, may consider, ascertain, adjust, determine, compromise, and settle any claim for money damages against the United States for injury or loss of property or personal injury or death caused by the negligent or wrongful act or omission of any employee of the agency while acting within the scope of his office or employment, under circumstances where the United States, if a private person, would be liable to the claimant in accordance with the law of the place where the act or omission occurred: Provided, That any award, compromise, or settlement in excess of $25,000 shall be effected only with the prior written approval of the Attorney General or his designee. Notwithstanding the proviso contained in the preceding sentence, any award, compromise, or settlement may be effected without the prior written approval of the Attorney General or his or her designee, to the extent that the Attorney General delegates to the head of the agency the authority to make such award, compromise, or settlement. Such delegations may not exceed the authority delegated by the Attorney General to the United States attorneys to settle claims for money damages against the United States. Each Federal agency may use arbitration, or other alternative means of dispute resolution under the provisions of subchapter IV of chapter 5 of title 5, to settle any tort claim against the United States, to the extent of the agency's authority to award, compromise, or settle such claim without the prior written approval of the Attorney General or his or her designee.

Subject to the provisions of this title relating to civil actions on tort claims against the United States, any such award, compromise, settlement, or determination shall be final and conclusive on all offices of the Government, except when procured by means of fraud. Any award, compromise, or settlement in an amount of $2,500 or less made pursuant to this section shall be paid by the head of the Federal agency concerned out of appropriations available to that agency. Payment of any award, compromise, or settlement in an amount in excess of $2,500 made pursuant to this section or made by the Attorney General in any amount pursuant to section 2677 of this title shall be paid in a manner similar to judgments and compromises in like causes and appropriations or funds available for the payment of such judgments and compromises are hereby made available for the payment of awards, compromises, or settlements under this chapter.

The acceptance by the claimant of any such award, compromise, or settlement shall be final and conclusive on the claimant, and shall constitute a complete release of any claim against the United States and against the employee of the government whose act or omission gave rise to the claim, by reason of the same subject matter.

Sec. 2673. Reports to Congress

The head of each federal agency shall report annually to Congress all claims paid by it under section 2672 of this title, stating the name of each claimant, the amount claimed, the amount awarded, and a brief description of the claim.

Sec. 2674. Liability of United States

The United States shall be liable, respecting the provisions of this title relating to tort claims, in the same manner and to the same extent as a private individual under like circumstances, but shall not be liable for interest prior to judgment or for punitive damages.

If, however, in any case wherein death was caused, the law of the place where the act or omission complained of occurred provides, or has been construed to provide, for damages only punitive in nature, the United States shall be liable for actual or compensatory damages, measured by the pecuniary injuries resulting from such death to the persons respectively, for whose benefit the action was brought, in lieu thereof.

With respect to any claim under this chapter, the United States shall be entitled to assert any defense based upon judicial or legislative immunity which otherwise would have been available to the employee of the United States whose act or omission gave rise to the claim, as well as any other defenses to which the United States is entitled.

With respect to any claim to which this section applies, the Tennessee Valley Authority shall be entitled to assert any defense which otherwise would have been available to the employee based upon judicial or legislative immunity, which otherwise would have been available to the employee of the Tennessee Valley Authority whose act or omission gave rise to the claim as well as any other defenses to which the Tennessee Valley Authority is entitled under this chapter.

Sec. 2675. Disposition by federal agency as prerequisite; evidence

(a) An action shall not be instituted upon a claim against the United States for money damages for injury or loss of property or personal injury or death caused by the negligent or wrongful act or omission of any employee of the Government while acting within the scope of his office or employment, unless the claimant shall have first presented the claim to the appropriate Federal agency and his claim shall have been finally denied by the agency in writing and sent by certified or registered mail. The failure of an agency to make final disposition of a claim within six months after it is filed shall, at the option of the claimant any time thereafter, be deemed a final denial of the claim for purposes of this section. The provisions of this subsection shall not apply to such claims as may be asserted under the Federal Rules of Civil Procedure by third party complaint, cross-claim, or counterclaim.

(b) Action under this section shall not be instituted for any sum in excess of the amount of the claim presented to the federal agency, except where the increased amount is based upon newly discovered evidence not reasonably discoverable at the time or presenting the claim to the federal agency, or upon allegation and proof of intervening facts, relating to the amount of the claim.

(c) Disposition of any claim by the Attorney General or other head of a federal agency shall not be competent evidence of liability or amount of damages.

Sec. 2676. Judgment as bar

The judgment in an action under section 1346 (b) of this title shall constitute a complete bar to any action by the claimant, by reason of the same subject matter, against the employee of the government whose act or omission gave rise to the claim.

Sec. 2677. Compromise

The Attorney General or his designee may arbitrate, compromise, or settle any claim cognizable under section 1346(b) of this title, after the commencement of an action thereon.

Sec. 2678. Attorney fees; penalty

No attorney shall charge, demand, receive, or collect for services rendered, fees in excess of 25 per centum of any judgment rendered pursuant to section 1346(b) of this title or any settlement made pursuant to section 2677 of this title, or in excess of 20 per centum of any award, compromise, or settlement made pursuant to section 2672 of this title. Any attorney who charges, demands, receives, or collects for services rendered in connection with such claim any amount in excess of that allowed under this section, if recovery be had, shall be fined not more than $2,000 or imprisoned not more than one year, or both.

Sec. 2679. Exclusiveness of remedy

(a) The authority of any federal agency to sue and be sued in its own name shall not be construed to authorize suits against such federal agency on claims which are cognizable under section 1346(b) of this title, and the remedies provided by this title in such cases shall be exclusive.

(b)(1) The remedy against the United States provided by sections 1346(b) and 2672 of this title for injury or loss of property, or personal injury or death arising or resulting from the negligent or wrongful act or omission of any employee of the Government while acting within the scope of his office or employment is exclusive of any other civil action or proceeding for money damages by reason of the same subject matter against the employee whose act or omission gave rise to the claim or against the estate of such employee. Any other civil action or proceeding for money damages arising out of or relating to the same subject matter against the employee or the employee's estate is precluded without regard to when the act or omission occurred.

(b)(2) Paragraph (1) does not extend or apply to a civil action against an employee of the Government—

(A) which is brought for a violation of the Constitution of the United States, or

(B) which is brought for a violation of a statute of the United States under which such action against an individual is otherwise authorized.

(c) The Attorney General shall defend any civil action or proceeding brought in any court against any employee of the Government or his estate for any such damage or injury. The employee against whom such civil action or proceeding is brought shall deliver within such time after date of service or knowledge of service as determined by the Attorney General, all process served upon him or an attested true copy thereof to his immediate superior or to whomever was designated by the head of his department to receive such papers and such person shall promptly furnish copies of the pleadings and process therein to the United States attorney for the district embracing the place wherein the proceeding is brought, to the Attorney General, and to the head of his employing Federal agency.

(d)(1) Upon certification by the Attorney General that the defendant employee was acting within the scope of his office or employment at the time of the incident out of which the claim arose, any civil action or proceeding commenced upon such claim in a United States district court shall be deemed an action against the United States under the provisions of this title and all references thereto, and the United States shall be substituted as the party defendant.

(d)(2) Upon certification by the Attorney General that the defendant employee was acting within the scope of his office or employment at the time of the incident out of which the claim arose, any civil action or proceeding commenced upon such claim in a State court shall be removed without bond at any time before trial by the Attorney General to the district court of the United States for the district and division embracing the place in which the action or proceeding is pending. Such action or proceeding shall be deemed to be an action or proceeding brought against the United States under the provisions of this title and all references thereto, and the United States shall be substituted as the party defendant. This certification of the Attorney General shall conclusively establish scope of office or employment for purposes of removal.

(d)(3) In the event that the Attorney General has refused to certify scope of office or employment under this section, the employee may at any time before trial petition the court to find and certify that the employee was acting within the scope of his office or employment. Upon such certification by the court, such action or proceeding shall be deemed to be an action or proceeding brought against the United States under the provisions of this title and all references thereto, and the United States shall be substituted as the party defendant. A copy of the petition shall be served upon the United States in accordance with the provisions of Rule 4(d)(4) of the Federal Rules of Civil Procedure. In the event the petition is filed in a civil action or proceeding pending in a State court, the action or proceeding may be removed without bond by the Attorney General to the district court of the United States for the district and division embracing the place in which it is pending. If, in considering the petition, the district court determines that the employee was not acting within the scope of his office or employment, the action or proceeding shall be remanded to the State court.

(d)(4) Upon certification, any action or proceeding subject to paragraph (1), (2), or (3) shall proceed in the same manner as any action against the United States filed pursuant to section 1346(b) of this title and shall be subject to the limitations and exceptions applicable to those actions.

(d)(5) Whenever an action or proceeding in which the United States is substituted as the party defendant under this subsection is dismissed for failure first to present a claim pursuant to section 2675(a) of this title, such a claim shall be deemed to be timely presented under section 2401(b) of this title if—

> (A) the claim would have been timely had it been filed on the date the underlying civil action was commenced, and (B) the claim is presented to the appropriate Federal agency within 60 days after dismissal of the civil action.

(e) The Attorney General may compromise or settle any claim asserted in such civil action or proceeding in the manner provided in section 2677, and with the same effect.

Sec. 2680. Exceptions

The provisions of this chapter and section 1346(b) of this title shall not apply to—

(a) Any claim based upon an act or omission of an employee of the Government, exercising due care, in the execution of a statute or regulation, whether or not such statute or regulation be valid, or based upon the exercise or performance or the failure to exercise or perform a discretionary function or duty on the part of a federal agency or an employee of the Government, whether or not the discretion involved be abused.

(b) Any claim arising out of the loss, miscarriage, or negligent transmission of letters or postal matter.

(c) Any claim arising in respect of the assessment or collection of any tax or customs duty, or the detention of any goods or merchandise by any officer of customs or excise or any other law-enforcement officer.

(d) Any claim for which a remedy is provided by sections 741-752, 781-790 of Title 46, relating to claims or suits in admiralty against the United States.

(e) Any claim arising out of an act or omission of any employee of the Government in administering the provisions of sections 1-31 of Title 50, Appendix.

(f) Any claim for damages caused by the imposition or establishment of a quarantine by the United States.

(g) Repealed. Sept. 26, 1950, ch. 1049, Sec. 13 (5), 64 Stat. 1043.)

(h) Any claim arising out of assault, battery, false imprisonment, false arrest, malicious prosecution, abuse of process, libel, slander, misrepresentation, deceit, or interference with contract rights: Provided, That, with regard to acts or omissions of investigative or law enforcement officers of the United States Government, the provisions of this chapter and section 1346(b) of this title shall apply to any claim arising, on or after the date of the enactment of this proviso, out of assault, battery, false imprisonment, false arrest, abuse of process, or malicious prosecution. For the purpose of this subsection, "investigative or law enforcement officer" means any officer of the United States who is empowered by law to execute searches, to seize evidence, or to make arrests for violations of Federal law.

(i) Any claim for damages caused by the fiscal operations of the Treasury or by the regulation of the monetary system.

(j) Any claim arising out of the combatant activities of the military or naval forces, or the Coast Guard, during time of war.

(k) Any claim arising in a foreign country.

(l) Any claim arising from the activities of the Tennessee Valley Authority.

(m) Any claim arising from the activities of the Panama Canal Company.

(n) Any claim arising from the activities of a Federal land bank, a Federal intermediate credit bank, or a bank for cooperatives.

APPENDIX 6:
SAMPLE NOTICE OF CLAIM

In the Matter of the Claim of

JOHN DOE, Claimant   NOTICE OF CLAIM

     -against-

THE NEW YORK CITY DEPARTMENT OF
TRANSPORTATION AND THE CITY OF
NEW YORK, Respondents

TO: THE NEW YORK CITY DEPARTMENT OF TRANSPORTATION
       THE CITY OF NEW YORK

SIRS:

PLEASE TAKE NOTICE that the claimant herein hereby makes a claim and demand against the City of New York, as follows:

    1. The name and post-office address of claimant and his attorney is:

        Claimant: John Doe
                 79-11 41st Avenue
                 Elmhurst, New York 11373

        Attorney: [Attorney Name]
                 [Attorney Address and Telephone Number]

    2. The nature of the claim is: Personal injuries sustained by claimant as a result of a fall caused by a large, deep and uneven depression located on a public street.

    3. The time, place and manner in which the claim arose: The incident complained of took place on October 19, 1999 at approximately 12:00 p.m. in the afternoon, on 43rd Avenue at the intersection of Bell Boulevard in the County of Queens, City of New York. Claimant was crossing the street in the crosswalk when he stepped immediately to the left of

the crosswalk to avoid a turning vehicle. Claimant stepped into the aforementioned depression and fell to the ground. Claimant was taken from the scene by ambulance to the hospital.

4. The items of damage claimed are: The Claimant sustained ankle injuries, including a severe ankle sprain and contusions, and has otherwise suffered bodily pain and suffering and emotional distress. Claimant is presently undergoing evaluation and treatment for said injuries thus, the extent of the damages are not presently knowable. Said claim and demand is hereby presented for adjustment and payment.

5. This notice is made and served on behalf of said infant in compliance with the provisions of Section 50-e of the General Municipal Law and such other laws and statutes as are in the case made and provided.

WHEREFORE, I respectfully request that this claim be allowed and paid by the said NYC Department of Transportation and The City of New York.

Dated: South Salem, NY
         November 15, 1999

                                    _____
                                    [Attorney Name/Address/Tel. No.]

TO: *Via Certified Mail*

        Office of the City Comptroller
        Bureau of Law and Adjustment
        1 Centre Street, Room 1220
        New York, New York 10007

GLOSSARY

Accrue To occur or come into existence.

Accuse To directly and formally institute legal proceedings against a person, charging that he or she has committed an offense.

Act of God Manifestation of the forces of nature which are unpredictable and difficult to anticipate, such as lightning and earthquakes.

Action at Law A judicial proceeding whereby one party prosecutes another for a wrong done.

Actionable Giving rise to a cause of action.

Actionable Negligence The breach or nonperformance of a legal duty through neglect or carelessness, resulting in damage or injury to another.

Actual Damages Actual damages are those damages directly referable to the breach or tortious act, and which can be readily proven to have been sustained, and for which the injured party should be compensated as a matter of right.

Ad Damnum Clause The clause in a complaint which sets forth the amount of damages demanded.

Adjudication The determination of a controversy and pronouncement of judgment.

Admissible Evidence	Evidence which may be received by a trial court to assist the trier of fact, either the judge or jury, in deciding a dispute.
Admission	The voluntary acknowledgment that certain facts are true.
Adversary	Opponent or litigant in a legal controversy or litigation.
Affirmative Defense	In a pleading, a matter constituting a defense.
Agency	The relationship between a principal and an agent who is employed by the principal, to perform certain acts dealing with third parties.
Agent	One who represents another known as the principal.
Amend	As in a pleading, to make an addition to, or a subtraction from, an already existing pleading.
Answer	In a civil proceeding, the principal pleading on the part of the defendant in response to the plaintiff's complaint.
Appeal	Resort to a higher court for the purpose of obtaining a review of a lower court decision.
Appearance	To come into court, personally or through an attorney, after being summoned.
Appellate Court	A court having jurisdiction to review the law as applied to a prior determination of the same case.
Argument	A discourse set forth for the purpose of establishing one's position in a controversy.
Assumption of Risk	The legal doctrine that a plaintiff may not recover for an injury to which he assents.
Breach of Duty	In a general sense, any violation or omission of a legal or moral duty.

Burden of Proof	The duty of a party to substantiate an allegation or issue to convince the trier of fact as to the truth of their claim.
Caption	The heading of a legal document which contains the name of the court, the index number assigned to the matter, and the names of the parties.
Cause of Action	The factual basis for bringing a lawsuit.
Circumstantial Evidence	Indirect evidence by which a principal fact may be inferred.
Citation	A reference to a source of legal authority, such as a case or statute.
Civil Action	An action maintained to protect a private, civil right as opposed to a criminal action.
Civil Court	The court designed to resolve disputes arising under the common law and civil statutes.
Civil Law	Law which applies to non-criminal actions.
Civil Penalty	A fine imposed as punishment for a certain activity.
Common Area	In landlord-tenant law, refers to the area of the premises which is used by all tenants, e.g. hallways, elevators, etc.
Compensatory Damages	Compensatory damages are those damages directly referable to a breach or tortious act, and which can be readily proven to have been sustained, and for which the injured party should be compensated as a matter of right.
Complaint	In a civil proceeding, the first pleading of the plaintiff setting out the facts on which the claim for relief is based.
Compromise and Settlement	An arrangement arrived at, either in court or out of court, for settling a dispute upon what appears to the parties to be equitable terms.

Conclusion of Fact	A conclusion reached by natural inference and based solely on the facts presented.
Conclusion of Law	A conclusion reached through the application of rules of law.
Conclusive Evidence	Evidence which is incontrovertible.
Consequential Damages	Consequential damages are those damages which are caused by an injury, but which are not a necessary result of the injury, and must be specially pleaded and proven in order to be awarded.
Contingency Fee	The fee charged by an attorney, which is dependent upon a successful outcome in the case, and is often agreed to be a percentage of the party's recovery.
Contributory Negligence	The act or omission amounting to want of ordinary care on the part of the complaining party which, concurring with the defendant's negligence, is the proximate cause of his or her injury.
Court	The branch of government responsible for the resolution of disputes arising under the laws.
Culpable	Referring to conduct, it is that which is deserving of moral blame.
Damages	In general, damages refers to monetary compensation which the law awards to one who has been injured by the actions of another, such as in the case of tortious conduct or breach of contractual obligations.
Defendant	In a civil proceeding, the party responding to the complaint.
Defense	Opposition to the truth or validity of the plaintiff's claims.
Discovery	Modern pretrial procedure by which one party gains information held by another party.

Dram Shop Act	Refers to laws which impose strict liability upon the seller of intoxicating beverages when harm is caused to a third party as a result of the sale.
Duty	The obligation, to which the law will give recognition and effect, to conform to a particular standard of conduct toward another.
Expert Witness	A witness who has special knowledge about a certain subject, upon which he or she will testify, which knowledge is not normally possessed by the average person.
Eyewitness	A person who can testify about a matter because of his or her own presence at the time of the event.
Fact Finder	In a judicial or administrative proceeding, the person, or group of persons, that has the responsibility of determining the acts relevant to decide a controversy.
Fact Finding	A process by which parties present their evidence and make their arguments to a neutral person, who issues a nonbinding report based on the findings, which usually contains a recommendation for settlement.
Finding	Decisions made by the court on issues of fact or law.
Foreseeability	A concept used to limit the liability of a party for the consequences of his or her acts, to consequences that are within the scope of a foreseeable risk.
Freedom of Information Act (FOIA)	A federal law which requires federal agencies to disclose information in its possession which is not exempt from the law.
General Damages	General damages are those damages directly referable to the breach or tortious act and which can be readily proven to have been sustained, and for which the injured party should be compensated as a matter of right.

Hearing	A proceeding during which evidence is taken for the purpose of determining the facts of a dispute and reaching a decision.
Illegal	Against the law.
Immunity	A benefit of exemption from a duty or penalty.
Inference	A reasoned deduction based on the given facts.
Injury	Any damage done to another's person, rights, reputation or property.
Insufficient Evidence	The judicial decision that the evidence submitted to prove a case does not meet the degree necessary to go forward with the action.
Insurance	A contingency agreement, supported by consideration, whereby the insured receives a benefit, e.g., money, in the event the contingency occurs.
Intentional Tort	A tort or wrong perpetrated by one who intends to do that which the law has declared wrong, as contrasted with negligence in which the tortfeasor fails to exercise that degree of care in doing what is otherwise permissible.
Invitee	One who enters another's property by invitation.
Joint and Several	The rights and liabilities shared among a group of people individually and collectively.
Judge	The individual who presides over a court, and whose function it is to determine controversies.
Judgment	A judgment is a final determination by a court of law concerning the rights of the parties to a lawsuit.
Jurisdiction	The power to hear and determine a case.
Jury	A group of individuals summoned to decide the facts in issue in a lawsuit.

Jury Trial	A trial during which the evidence is presented to a jury so that they can determine the issues of fact, and render a verdict based upon the law as it applies to their findings of fact.
Liability	Liability refers to one's obligation to do or refrain from doing something, such as the payment of a debt.
License	A privilege to perform some act upon the land of another without possessing any estate therein.
Licensee	A licensee upon one's land is one who is privileged to enter or remain on the land only by virtue of the landowner's consent.
Municipal Corporation	Generally refers to incorporated cities, towns and villages.
Negligence	The failure to exercise that degree of care which a person of ordinary prudence would exercise under the same circumstances. Refers to conduct which falls below the standard established by law for the protection of others against unreasonable risk of harm.
Negligence Per Se	Conduct, whether of action or omission, which may be declared and treated as negligence without any argument or proof as to the particular surrounding circumstances, because it is contrary to the law.
Nominal Damages	A trivial sum of money which is awarded as recognition that a legal injury was sustained, although slight.
Nuisance	The disturbance of another's use of their property, rendering continued use uncomfortable or inconvenient.
Occupational Safety and Health Act (OSHA)	A law passed by Congress in 1970 to protect employees from injury or illness in the course of their employment by enforcing safety and health standards.

Offense	Any misdemeanor or felony violation of the law for which a penalty is prescribed.
Ordinance	A local law passed by a municipal legislative body.
Ordinary Care	The care a reasonably careful person would use under similar circumstances using diligence and exercise of good judgment.
Pain and Suffering	Refers to damages recoverable against a wrongdoer which include physical or mental suffering.
Parties	The disputants.
Plaintiff	In a civil proceeding, the one who initially brings the lawsuit.
Prima Facie Case	A case which is sufficient on its face, being supported by at least the requisite minimum of evidence, and being free from palpable defects.
Provocation	The act of inciting another to do a particular deed.
Proximate Cause	That which, in a natural and continuous sequence, unbroken by any efficient intervening cause, produces injury, and without which the result would not have occurred.
Punitive Damages	Compensation in excess of compensatory damages which serves as a form of punishment to the wrongdoer who has exhibited malicious and willful misconduct.
Question of Fact	The fact in dispute which is the province of the trier of fact, i.e., the judge or jury, to decide.
Question of Law	The question of law which is the province of the judge to decide.
Release	A document signed by one party, releasing claims he or she may have against another party, usually as part of a settlement agreement.
Relief	The remedies afforded a complainant by the court.

Remedy	Refers to the means by which a right is enforced or a violation of a right is compensated.
Respondent	The responding party, also known as the defendant.
Restatement of the Law	A series of volumes authored by the American Law Institute that tell what the law in a general area is, how it is changing, and what direction the authors think this change should take.
Retainer Agreement	A contract between an attorney and the client stating the nature of the services to be rendered and the cost of the services.
Service of Process	The delivery of legal court documents, such as a complaint, to the defendant.
Settlement	An agreement by the parties to a dispute on a resolution of the claims, usually requiring some mutual action, such as payment of money in consideration of a release of claims.
Sovereign Immunity	A doctrine which prohibits lawsuits against the government without its consent.
Statute of Limitations	Any law which fixes the time within which parties must take judicial action to enforce rights or thereafter be barred from enforcing them.
Subpoena	A court issued document compelling the appearance of a witness before the court.
Summary Judgment	A judgment of the court which disposes of a controversy, based upon a motion brought by one of the parties, which demonstrates that there are no existing factual disputes in issue which necessitate a jury determination.
Summons	A mandate requiring the appearance of the defendant in an action under penalty of having judgment entered against him for failure to do so.
Testify	The offering of a statement in a judicial proceeding, under oath and subject to the penalty of perjury.

Testimony	The sworn statement make by a witness in a judicial proceeding.
Tort	A private or civil wrong or injury, other than breach of contract, for which the court will provide a remedy in the form of an action for damages.
Tort Claims Act	A statute passed by Congress which waives the government's sovereign immunity from tort liability.
Tortfeasor	A wrong-doer.
Tortious Conduct	Wrongful conduct, whether of act or omission, of such a character as to subject the actor to liability under the law of torts.
Trespass	A tortious interference with another's property.
Trespasser	An individual who enters upon another's property without the owner's permission.
Trial	The judicial procedure whereby disputes are determined based on the presentation of issues of law and fact. Issues of fact are decided by the trier of fact, either the judge or jury, and issues of law are decided by the judge.
Trial Court	The court of original jurisdiction over a particular matter.
Ultrahazardous	In tort law, refers to an activity which involves such a risk of harm to individuals or their property, that it gives rise to strict liability for any damage caused as a result of the activity.
Verdict	The definitive answer given by the jury to the court concerning the matters of fact committed to the jury for their deliberation and determination.
Vicarious Liability	In tort law, refers to the liability assessed against one party due to the actions of another party.

BIBLIOGRAPHY AND SUGGESTED READING

American Bar Association (Date Visited: June 2000) <http://www.abanet.org).

Black's Law Dictionary, Fifth Edition. St. Paul, MN: West Publishing Company, 1979.

National Center for Injury Prevention and Control (Date Visited: June 2000) <http://www.ncipc.org>.

National Safety Council (Date Visited: June 2000) <http://www.nsc.org>.

Rojak, Lawrence N. *New York Insurance and Negligence Digest*. Costa Mesa, CA: James Publishing, Inc., 1999.

Shayne, Neil T. *Winning the "Slip and Fall" Case*. New York, NY: Practising Law Institute, 1989.

Turnbow, Charles E. *Slip & Fall Practice*. Costa Mesa, CA: James Publishing, Inc., 1999.

For Reference

Not to be taken from this room